THEATRE SYM
A PUBLICATION OF THE SOUTHEASTERN

Drama as Rhetoric/Rhetoric as Drama

An Exploration of Dramatic and Rhetorical Criticism

Volume 5

Published by the

Southeastern Theatre Conference and

The University of Alabama Press

THEATRE SYMPOSIUM is published annually by the Southeastern Theatre Conference, Inc. (SETC), and by The University of Alabama Press. SETC nonstudent members receive the journal as a part of their membership under rules determined by SETC. For information on membership, write to SETC, P.O. Box 9868, Greensboro, NC 27429-0868. All other inquiries regarding subscriptions, circulation, purchase of individual copies, and requests to reprint materials should be addressed to The University of Alabama Press, Box 870380, Tuscaloosa, AL 35487-0380.

THEATRE SYMPOSIUM publishes works of scholarship resulting from a single-topic meeting held on a southeastern university campus each spring. A call for papers to be presented at that meeting is widely publicized each autumn for the following spring. Authors are therefore not encouraged to send unsolicited manuscripts directly to the editor. Information about the next symposium is available from the editor, Stanley V. Longman, Department of Drama, University of Georgia, Athens, Georgia 30602-3154.

THEATRE SYMPOSIUM
A PUBLICATION OF THE SOUTHEASTERN THEATRE CONFERENCE

Volume 5   1997

Contents

Introduction

HIS VOLUME OF the *Theatre Symposium* deals with a topic that
has strong classical associations: the fascinating aesthetic and
social connection between drama and rhetoric. The Greek world was
fully alive to this connection, having begun to explore the terrain as
early as the sixth century B.C. And naturally, one thinks immediately
of fourth-century Aristotle, whose *Rhetoric* formed a tight companion
to his *Poetics*. Interest in the shared issues between drama and rhetoric
was renewed with the Renaissance, and indeed many of the ideas advanced by neoclassicism merge rhetorical concepts into dramatic theory.
Yet the eighteenth, nineteenth, and early twentieth centuries generally
ignored the kinship between the two. In our own time, such theorists
as Kenneth Burke, Ernest Bowman, Elder Olson, and Paul de Man have
rekindled our interest in the rhetorical dimension of drama and in the
dramatic nature of rhetoric. Both, after all, concern themselves with
the process of affecting audiences. Both are founded on the notion of
society, any audience being a compendium of its society, a public in
miniature, whose gathering cannot help but imply the larger world existing outside the hall or theatre.

The papers appearing in this volume were selected from those originally presented at a conference held in Columbia at the University of
South Carolina, April 19–21, 1996. That conference, organized and
hosted by Charles Wilbanks and Steven Hart, both of the Department
of Theatre, Speech and Dance of the University of South Carolina,
occasioned a lively exchange of ideas among scholars from many different disciplines: speech communication, drama, English literature, comparative literature, classics, and romance languages and literature. The

conference also included a performance of works out of the Harlem Renaissance and a panel discussion of the issues raised in those works.

The editorial board helped in the selection of the papers to be published in this volume. The essays fall into four categories that correspond to the four parts of this publication. The first part sets the classical backdrop for the discussion, introducing new insights into the ways in which rhetoric informs the dramatic experience by re-examining the Greek context. Two of these papers, one by August Staub, the other by Tom Heeney, explore the rhetorical dimension of drama on theoretical grounds. The third, by John Arthos, puts into perspective the rhetorical elements of a specific Greek play, *The Suppliants* of Aeschylus. Part two addresses the Renaissance and neoclassical periods, with Maria Galli Stampino's essay on the epideictic nature of the Pastoral in Renaissance Italy, George Geckle's comparison of Shakespeare's rhetoric with the ideology presented in Ian McKellen's *Richard III,* and Odai Johnson's views of the rhetorical in Thomas Otway's play *Venice Preserv'd.* Part three brings the theatre into the context of war and politics, where the rhetorical character of drama is explored in three instances: the political arena of the Federalists and the Republicans in the 1790s, which Steve Wilmer examines in his essay on plays staged in that time; the political implications behind the popular stage versions of *Uncle Tom's Cabin,* described by Charles Wilbanks; and the modern Italian political warfare apparent in Dario Fo's "angry farces" in Stanley Longman's essay. Finally, part four introduces two essays that examine the rhetorical dimensions of drama in the context of contemporary culture: Leigh Anne Howard explores the nature of the deconstruction an audience experiences in Beckett's dramaturgy, and Peter Michael Pober analyzes the culture surrounding AIDS and the plays of Larry Kramer.

In editing this volume, I owe special thanks to the members of the editorial board, to associate editor Steven Hart, and to my assistants here at the University of Georgia, Ryan Ritter and Mick Sokol. In addition, I am indebted to the two previous editors, Philip Hill and Paul Castagno for their valuable advice. Finally, I am grateful to the contributors to this volume for their excellent work and for their help in the editing process.

STANLEY VINCENT LONGMAN
Editor

The Enthymeme and the Invention

of Troping in Greek Drama

August W. Staub

E CITIZENS OF the *fin de siècle* are defined by our privacy. Given a choice between valuing the group or the
private individual, we choose the individual. It is difficult, then, for us
to realize that the ancient Greeks placed very little value on the individual and no value whatsoever on private matters. As James Redfield
points out, we have scant informal evidence from ancient Greek culture:
"We have instead, formal representations: shaped and painted images,
literary narratives, historical accounts, philosophic analyses, and public
speeches. . . . We meet the Greeks, as it were, in their Sunday best; we
do not catch them unawares but see them as they chose to represent
themselves. These representations, further, are with few exceptions representations of public life" (1995, 153).

It is with the very publicness of the ancient Greeks that I wish to
deal and with the implications of that publicness in ancient theatre.
Although public activity is various and extensive,[1] my special concern
is with public as opposed to private *thought*. When presenting thought
in his *Poetics*, Aristotle uses the term *dianoia*, and he refers us to his

---

[1]Ritual and religious ceremony is usually a public event. Even eating can be public, as
in sacrificial eating (See Detienne and Vernant 1989) or in *symposia* (see *Greek Symposia,*
Michael Vickers, Joint Association of Classic Teachers, London, n.d.). Athletics, of course,
were great public events (See *Greek Athletes and Athletics,* London, 1984). Warfare in the
Greek practice was an especially public act. The phalanx was entirely dependent on the
civic commitment of each warrior.

work on rhetoric, to which he says the issue of thought properly belongs (Aristotle 1951, XIX, 2).

In the *Rhetoric*, Aristotle makes clear immediately that rhetoric is a type of thinking—the counterpart of dialectic (1921, I, 2)—but it is not concerned with what seems logical to an individual but what seems logical to a given class (1921, I, 2). That is, rhetoric is concerned with public thinking, *phronesis*, or the practical thought processes common to a given civic order. As such, rhetoric is characterized by the *enthymeme*, a thought process used by the group, as opposed to formal logic. Because Aristotle gives no further definition, the traditional assumption has been that the *enthymeme* is some sort of faulty syllogism, but the new rhetoricians of the second half of this century have taken issue with such an assumption.[2] As Eugene Garver points out in his recent and illuminating study of the *Rhetoric*, we cannot define the *enthymeme* as "a syllogism with defective or probable premises or with a missing premise" (1994, 150). Indeed, Aristotle is quite clear that just as there are false or illogical syllogisms in dialectic, there are also false or sham *enthymemes* (1951, II, 23–25). The *enthymeme* is not poor or secondary logic but, as Garver observes, the process of thought employed by a "civic intelligence" (34).

The whole force of classical Greek culture was toward the perfection of civic life; so it is small wonder that Aristotle felt no compulsion to defend the value of the *enthymeme* or to engage in lengthy definition. Of the nature of the *enthymeme* he says only that it must not employ long chains of reasoning or it will lose clarity, nor should it include every link else it fall into prolixity (1951, II, 22).

But there is considerably more to the *enthymeme* than brevity. To understand the complexity of the *enthymeme*, we must see it as suasion in action in ancient Greek culture. And where might we go to observe the *enthymeme* at play? Why to the only complete surviving examples of public life in ancient Greece: the *dramenon* of the city-wide festivals, frequently cited by Aristotle himself. Unquestionably, in the works intended for performance in the Greek theatre the method was to present public figures (kings, queens, potentates, gods) thinking and act-

---

[2]Led by the work of Kenneth Burke (*Rhetoric of Motives*, Berkeley, 1958), the new rhetoric movement has done much to reclaim the importance of rhetoric as something deeper than mere decorative language. Some recent basic works of the new rhetoricians include E. L. Bowie's *The Importance of the Sophists*, New Haven, 1982; B. Vicker's *In Defense of Rhetoric*, Oxford, 1988; J. Fernandez's *Persuasions and Performances*, Bloomington, 1986; and *The Social Uses of Metaphor: Essays in the Anthropology of Rhetoric*, edited by J. C. Crocker and J. D. Sapir, Philadelphia, 1977.

ing publicly to encourage a public thought process in the spectators. Greek plays are not "kitchen dramas" but events of the civic assembly. They are organized around a chorus that represents the civic order of the play, and they are presented at public festivals before spectators who are very aware of each other's presence in a sunlit and open seeing place, the *theatron*. Indeed, the very seeing place itself is crucial to all Greek thinking, for as Charles Segal and others point out: "The Greeks are a race of spectators" (Segal 1995, 184). To see a thing is to understand that thing. The Greek word *"theoria* implies the same identification of knowledge with sight as that expressed in the common verb to know *oida* (of the root *vid*—to see)" (Segal 1995, 193).

Moreover, the dramas were the first public events in which myth was used enthymemically, as a rational device for a public assemblage. Of course, the epic preceded the drama, and the *rhapsode* was also presenting myth in a public assemblage. But the art of the *rhapsode* is based on example, a string of examples, not on the *enthymeme*. Indeed, Aristotle clearly differentiates in the *Rhetoric* between the *enthymeme* and the example (1951, II, 19–20). In fact, although he roughly classifies the example as inductive and the *enthymeme* as deductive, the difference lies more in the dynamics of the thought process. The *enthymeme,* particularly in drama, entails twisting ideas together in a nonlinear action. Reasoning from example, as in the epic, requires a linear procedure and thus a longer chain of reasoning—the very thing Aristotle cautions against in rhetorical argument. Indeed, the Greeks recognized the difference between linear thought—*logos*—and the more supple and more active and twisted practical thought—*metis* (Detienne and Vernant 1991, 3–4), a difference that today might be drawn between binary choices and a more fluid, more quantum suasion.

The maker of a *dramenon* was a transition agent. On the one hand, he was a *logo-graphien,* a writer of stories engaged in the structuring of narratives, but unlike those of the epic maker, his narratives were for the sighted and therefore immediately-knowing group. *Dramas* are for spectators, not audiences, and as a consequence they are enthymemic and mythic. As with any myth, they are to be grasped as a thing-in-action, which serves as singular proof of the thing's own validity because it is *seen* to be. Indeed, as Aristotle points out, the *mythos* is the soul of the *dramenon,* just as the *enthymeme* is the soul of rhetoric. It is my contention that the two are the same and that the *mythos* of drama may be called the dramatic *enthymeme.*

What is the nature of the dramatic *mythos* that makes it identical with the rhetorical *enthymeme*? Like the rhetorical *enthymeme,* dramatic *mythos* begins close to the point of suasion so that its action will not be obscure, and like the rhetorical *enthymeme*, it does not fill in all the links so that it may be brief. Most important, however, the dramatic *enthymeme* is always a trope. That is, the dramatic *enthymeme* always presents two or more actions turned in upon themselves. This turning inward is the *stasis* (Aristotle also uses the term *peripeteia* or turn around). The most common meaning for the term *stasis* is civil war, and like war the dramatic *stasis* is not a fixed point, as it will become in Roman thought, but a collection of agonistic energies (*dynamos*), a dynamic event that holds in tension the actions of the *prostasis* and the *exstasis* (ecstasy) so that the entire movement may be seen altogether, just as we currently perceive the universe in quantum terms. That is why it is appropriate to call the dramatic *enthymeme* a trope—a turning upon or twisting about. All *mythoi* in drama are so constructed.

Agamemnon's sacrifice of his daughter is finally twisted together with his own sacrifice by Clytemnestra. Indeed, the very *peripeteia* that entwines the two killings is a public and entirely visual event—Agamemnon's removing of some sort of footgear and his treading barefoot on some sort of sacred carpet. It was a very public spectacle of great potency to be grasped by the civic intelligence of the assembled Greek spectators. We sense that some powerful energy is at work, but it is no longer convincing to us. It is not our *enthymeme* but theirs.

In the twining or braiding together of the existing assumptions of a given cultural group, the suasion of the *enthymeme* occurs. On the simplest metaphorical or metonymic level we can see the *enthymeme* at work in such phrases as "Richard the Lion Hearted" or "Naturally his brother defended him; one hand washes the other, doesn't it?" In the one *enthymeme*, we literally argue that a particular English king was brave because we have twisted together his name, the part of his body considered to be the source of such qualities, and the image of a lion. This is a brief but extremely complex trope that calls for considerable mental agility. In the other example, we argue that families are as inseparable as the cooperating hands of a single body. But let us imagine a culture without the concept "lion": for example, a group living two hundred years ago in the Arctic. These people would draw no conclusion from the joining of Richard's heart with a lion. We could also postulate a culture that for religious reasons immobilized the left hand and arm. For this particular civic order, our second phrase would be illogical. Neither group should be considered unintelligent because they were not affected by one of the tropes. On the other hand, we should be cautious in assuming that tropes are faulty or simplistic thought. They may well be classified as the highest order of thought, even though they depend on a civic and not a singular intelligence.

Indeed, it is precisely because troping, the fundamental *enthymeme,* is so complex and agile, exactly because it involves the apprehension and joining of energy and motion in its very structure, that it must grow out of a public and civic intelligence. Consider the complicated web of entwined events that make up the stunning and disturbing *enthymeme* known as *Oedipus Tyrannus.* First there is the act of abandoning the infant to prevent his murdering his father, enfolded with the action of the grown son fleeing his home to escape his murdering his father, twisted with the action of his inadvertently killing his father, entwined with his unwittingly marrying his mother and having children by her— children who are his own brothers and sisters. This whole trope is enmeshed within itself even as the narrative of the *dramenon* begins so that it is an active helix turning endlessly upon itself, imploding throughout the short play. Indeed, the most significant event of the *dramenon* proper is the *stasis* or civil war between Oedipus and Jocasta in which she realizes that public shame is inevitable and commits suicide. Following his vision of his dead mother, Oedipus explodes the *stasis* into a public ecstacy of sorrow. The final suasive twist by which the whole trope is displayed is Oedipus embracing his own siblings as his children. The poet's intent is to persuade the spectators to pity and terror, because they see the final explosion of the complicated trope which they knew—from their cultural assumptions—could not forever implode. This logic of implosion/explosion, of tension and release, is the logic of the trope. Moreover tropic logic consists in equal parts of past—and therefore proven—events entwined with present actions, forming a single complex presented in a seeable whole movement.

The great achievement of the Greek dramatic poets, what raises them above the epic poet in the estimation of Aristotle, is the fashioning of the dramatic trope—the twisting about of images in an implosion-explosion turn-about—that is the very essence of public thought. That creation depends in great part on the facility of sight and therefore is especially the province of theatre—the art of the seeing place.

In the history of dramatic art since the Greeks, not all writers have elected to employ the dramatic *enthymeme.* Some works are tropic; some are not. And, of course, the variations wrung on the dramatic trope are endless. Among historical examples that come to mind are the medieval cycle plays in which heaven, earth, and hell are constantly twisted together in a single trope or in which past time and future time are turned upon one another, as in the *Second Shepherds's Play.* Shakespeare literally "tropes" his scenes into existence, calling upon "a muse of fire" and letting us *see* the outrageous comedy of a Roslyn played by a boy actor, disguising himself as a female character who then disguises herself as a

boy and then pretends to be a girl to show her sweetheart how he should
behave with her if she were actually present as a girl. What an elaborate
torque! What a wild trope! What we do see and think as public thought!

With the advent of the well-made play in the mid-nineteenth century, however, tropic structure was replaced by probability and linearity. Popular melodramas, as well as the more elite but equally melodramatic plays of Ibsen or Strindberg, depended on establishing a strong
set of present circumstances out of which an inciting incident prompted
a long chain of detailed events, each embodying binary choices and thus
each the consequence of its precedent. Such plays are logical, not
mythic. They are atropic. Twentieth-century interest in the interior life
of the individual presented the theatre with a peculiar problem. The
one is not the many. How, in a completely public art, can the intimate
life of the individual be presented for public consideration? Writers came
to employ again the tropic devices of the Greeks. From Strindberg's
Ghost Sonata to Caryl Churchill's *Cloud Nine,* from films such as *Citizen
Kane* to musicals such as *Cats,* the fundamental structure of modern
and especially postmodern drama has been tropic.

Detailed discussion of the kind and quality of each tropic attempt,
how it fits within the enthymemic structure of its culture, is the burden
of a much longer work. The point here is that we recognize the lasting
achievement of the Greek dramatists who fashioned the defining structure of the *enthymeme:* the dramatic trope. If we are ever tempted to
dismiss the logic of the *enthymeme* and the power of its informing impetus—the dramatic trope—we have but to remind ourselves of its
continuing vigor not only in the theatre but in all of Western thought.
Perhaps the most significant idea of the late twentieth century is that of
DNA as the structure of life itself. And how is that DNA thought about
but as a double helix—a dramatic trope!

Works Cited

Aristotle. 1951. *The Art of Poetry.* Trans. Philip Wheelwright. New York: Odys-
    sey Press.
———. 1921. *The Rhetoric.* Trans. Lane Cooper. New York: D. Appleton Cen-
    tury Company.
Boardman, John, Jasper Griffin, and Oswyn Murray. 1986. *The Oxford History
    of the Classical World.* Oxford: Oxford University Press.
Caspo, Eric, and William J. Slater. 1994. *The Context of Ancient Drama.* Ann
    Arbor: University of Michigan Press.
Detienne, Marcel, and Jean-Pierre Vernant. 1991. *Cunning Intelligence in*

Greek Society and Culture. Trans. Janet Lloyd. Chicago: University of Chicago Press.

———. 1989. *The Cuisine of Sacrifice among the Greeks.* Chicago: University of Chicago Press.

Garver, Eugene. 1994. *Aristotle's Rhetoric: An Art of Character.* Chicago: University of Chicago Press.

Redfield, James. 1995. "Homo Domesticus." In *The Greeks,* ed. Jean Pierre Vernant, trans. Charles Lamber and Teresa Lavender Fagan, 153–83. Chicago: University of Chicago Press.

Scodel, Ruth, ed. 1993. *Theatre and Society in the Classical World.* Ann Arbor: University of Michigan Press.

Segal, Charles. 1995. "Spectator and Listener." In *The Greeks,* ed. Jean Pierre Vernant, trans. Charles Lamber and Teresa Lavender Fagan, 184–217. Chicago: University of Chicago Press.

Theorizing the Spectacle

A Rhetorical Analysis of Tragic Recognition

Tom Heeney

I

*D*ESPITE THE EFFORTS of thinkers from Plato to Nietzsche, Freud, and Foucault to capture the essence of tragedy, it remains an enigma, a *terra incognita*. Tragedy is notoriously difficult to incorporate within theoretical models. The would-be "disinterested" spectator remains blind to vital dimensions of tragic consciousness, for the tragic voice is always enthralling, usually multivocal, often indeterminate, and traditionally inflected by issues of gender and authority (see Zeitlin 1990).

Aristotle's *Poetics* seeks to rationalize the power and stabilize the implications of tragedy and, by reading it with a philosophic eye, to domesticate its uncanny and unruly nature. As our first known systematic theory of tragedy, the *Poetics* attempts to impose an analytic unity of vision on a culturally unstable phenomenon. In this interpretive process, "tragic man" becomes a stranger and almost fades away behind the triumph of a new literary vision of tragedy (see Vernant and Vidal-Naquet 1988). In *Tragedy and Theory,* Michelle Gellrich reminds us that in "assuming a panoptic view of the field, the theorist seeks to master the material at his disposal and thus lay claim to authority" (1988, xi).

Aristotle is certainly such an influential authority. Of all the structural devices he identifies to account for the cultural power and rhetorical energy of tragedy as staged during the ancient festival of the Great Dionysia, the issue of recognition is clearly the most important. For Aristotle, it informs the tragic spectacle itself while relating tragedy to extradramatic topics. Theory may indeed bring insight, but it may also blind us to significant aspects of the experience of tragedy. We can nevertheless turn the issue of recognition into a critical lens to focus on tragedy's many rhetorical, psychological, social, and philosophical dimensions.

The question of recognition—*anagnorisis* in the original Greek—has a long tradition in drama, literature, philosophy; in more modern thought it figures prominently in psychoanalysis. That long tradition has produced centrifugal forces out of widening cultural convictions and interpretative methods. By this route, we have come face to face with what Terence Cave calls the "scandal of recognition" (see Cave 1990). Yet tragedy itself works centripetally, bringing together various social and psychic forces typifying a time and place, concentrating the *energeia* (energy) of seen and backstage tendencies, and putting a human face (*ethos*) on otherwise disembodied energies. The tragic spectacle dramatizes these tensions and contradictions and so helps an audience visualize what they must face as citizens and persons. And, as we shall see, the contemporary theorist must account for this same cohesive yet disruptive interplay of forces in tragedy.

As Aristotle recognized, plot (*muthos*) works as the soul of tragedy; narrative arrangements of action bring us to recognize who we are and our place in the social landscape. The plot binds together these otherwise disjointed and amorphous forces and so condenses issues in striking ways. Where otherwise blind chance or deaf necessity would reign, the plot manages to secure meaning. In general, drama fills a need when people sense a loss of historical moorings and secure meanings, as Alvin Gouldner comments: "The dramaturgic view of life arises when experience is losing its continuity and is dissolving into episodic shreds, when the larger architecture of experience is crumbling, when the rhythm and movement of life sprawls and lacks organizing centers or familiar punctuations and accents" (1971, 222). Thus dramaturgical strategies offer counterpoints to chaos. We must take care, however, to address the fifth century phenomenon of Attic theatre on its own terms rather than to view it through a Cartesian or a Freudian lens. The former would relate recognition to the *cogito*, the latter to psychological insight.

This paper seeks to show how the problem of recognition relates to the shift in the ancient world from an oral to a literate society. Tragedy as a civic institution maintains a delicate balance between myth and philosophy, dramatic performance and abstract theory. This cognitive and cultural transformation will be interpreted through the classical rhetorical *topoi* of *audience, situation,* and *ecphrasis.* The focal issue will be how recognition negotiates these historical tensions by animating opposing cultural modalities of communication. As Charles Segal suggests in an examination of Euripides' masterful use of the recognition scene, "the medium of recognition is a discourse about messages and about the relative values of writing and speech as secure and accurate modes of communication" (1986, 102).

Greek tragedy is generally considered a transitional cultural phenomenon, emerging at the moment when archaic oral epics recalling a collective mythic past were being superseded by written texts of playwrights and the abstract and literate speculations of philosophers. Attic theatre illustrates vividly how these communicative modes were put into play. The political shift from an aristocratic to a democratic society and the emerging philosophic distinction between appearance and reality took on visual and vivid dimensions when presented upon the tragic, self-conscious stage set before the *theatron* or "seeing place," as writing "accompanies that increasing acknowledgment of complexity in the vision of self and world which marks the fifth century" (Segal 1986, 82). Segal summarizes the significance of this delicate yet decisive moment when tragedy emerged from *mythos:* "The division in the philosophers, historians, and the tragic poets between surface and depth, appearance and reality, is encouraged by the special status of the written text in a hitherto oral culture. These authors have before them two modes of mental organization. Oral communication faces outward, to the interactive contextual space between speaker and audience; written communication faces inward, toward the personal relation with the hearer. Its concern is syntactics rather than pragmatics" (1986, 88–89).

Since Aristotle, however, recognition has been theorized primarily through the lens of literacy. This abstraction from performance and the visual staging of the tragic spectacle in its original context blinds us to an important rhetorical dimension of tragedy. Tragic rhetoric, I shall argue, should be recognized as an immediate and vivid "setting before the eyes" that allows the spectator to visualize one's life in the context of the cosmic spectacle. Recognition then becomes a matter of discovering the hidden reality of the interior life of emotions and experiences. The outward staging of tragedy allowed the assembled spectators to recognize the inner scene of personhood. This was a wondrous discovery, not of the Cartesian *cogito* or "I," for tragedy employed no word for "self," but rather of an awakened interiorized seeing through tragic spectacle (Segal 1986, 99). This newly introspective gaze coincides with the growing practice of reading. The world seen on stage and abstractly theorized for oneself by reading replaces the aural realm of the epic. The eye replaces the ear as our primary communicative link with the past and those here and now (see Havelock 1982). As Theodor Gomperz remarks in his classic work, *Greek Thinkers,* the "Greeks were naturally keen-sighted" (1901, 11).

II

In antiquity, the striking phenomenon that was tragic theatre joins the nature of the visible to the experience of *wonder* and *theory: "Theatron,* 'theatre,' is a space for beholding, derived from the verb *theaomai,* to behold with wonder" (Segal 1986, 75). The action on display before one's eyes also engages the assembled public in contemplation. Thus it places the meaning of the dramatic event both on stage and within a collective consciousness (*theoria*). Theorizing the visual spectacle of tragedy from the viewpoint of philosophy as Aristotle did, however, turns us away from the face-to-face encounters typical of an oral culture and requires we rethink meaning as mental spectacle in the sense of an abstract intellectual picture displayed before the mind's eye. This semantic and epistemic shift was neither simple nor smooth, as we shall see.

Among the pre-Socratics, the archaic term *kosmos* epitomized the whole. It assumed the possibility of grasping the essential relatedness of the cosmic order; here archaic thought saw a relationship between wonder, beauty, and the divine. Ernesto Grassi suggests that *kosmos* "refers in an ontological perspective to the 'relationship' between particular parts and the whole" (1980, 91). The term suggests a connection between immediate imagistic beauty and the more detached intellectual activity of comprehending the cosmic order. As a striking metaphor of this wondrous relationship, *kosmos* "presupposes a 'vision' of something hitherto concealed" (33). The ritual origins of drama also suggest that within the *theatron* one came face to face with gods (*theos*), and so experienced the revelation of ultimate powers (see Wilshire 1982, 33).

Tragedy as a dramatic and microcosmic spectacle, then, emerged at a transitional moment in history to symbolize an equally equivocal sense of things and to suggest the ultimate elusiveness of truth for the purely theoretical vision. For the appearance of classical tragedy coincided with decisive changes in the reciprocal development of narrative, history, religion, legislation, and the public arena, of which theatre was one significant part. A primarily literate *theoria* or narrative line allowed Plato, for example, to stage the famous and decisive confrontation in Book 10 of *The Republic* between the poets and philosophers.

But this increasingly abstract form of thinking relied on the predominance of written forms of communication (Segal 1986). The gradual shift from oral (rhapsodic) performance to writing also coincided with a recognition of the right of the common populace to *oversee* the judgment of public truths (Vernant 1982, 120). This emerging sense of openness conflicted with the mystery that religions and cults continued to practice by hiding their secrets from the eyes of the masses. The popularity of the dramatic theatre of Dionysos also parallels the emergence of silent reading within the intelligentsia at large and with it the discovery in antiquity of an "interior voice" (Svenbro 1990, 369). The *agora* and *theatron* together opened the communal space of the public arena, and this outward face on display allowed assembled spectators to contemplate the otherwise unseen, interior elements animating character (*ethos*) and law (*nomos*) (Havelock 1982, 264).

Tragedy emerged as a graphic communal and spatial form to dramatize the need for *isonomia*, or a balancing of tensions, in this case checking the influence of private activities through the oversight of the public spectacle. Yet philosophy in particular maintains an equivocal relation with writing and privacy, as Socrates reminds us in Plato's *Phaedrus*. Indeed, a young Plato symbolically burned his early attempts at writing tragedy in front of the Theatre of Dionysos at Socrates' suggestion! (Svenbro 1990, 379).

III

Plato develops a significant thematic connection between sunlight, personal sight and insight, and human intelligence. Taking up themes already in circulation, *The Republic* presents Plato's famous analogy relating the power of image-making, the ability of being seen, and the conditions of intelligibility for the mind's eye: being and truth become the intellectual lights making whatever can be known visible and manifest for inspection (see Sallis 1986). The cosmic order thus presented for inspection and contemplation was visualized as a mental spectacle for the philosophical gaze. This new form of speculative thought purportedly offered a greater explanatory power than the mythos it would supersede (see Vernant 1982).

Following John Sallis's masterful analysis of *The Republic*, we can see how the basic perceptual experience of *light* and *dark* join with the primary propositions of showing (what has visible distinctness) and hiding (what remains indeterminate). In the Platonic vision, knowing is described as a kind of self-showing, an experience of what becomes visible or comes into the open (*alethia*); knowing refers to what moves from being hidden to being open to human understanding. Knowledge, as it were, comes to light through verbal images, showing itself so that our understanding may clearly grasp the truth of the things we see. But then images for Plato, ironically enough, involve concealment. They present the mere semblance of things.

Philosophical understanding becomes *personal* insight: *eidenai* (knowing) and *idein* (seeing) are cognate, since knowing was thought of as a form of vision (see Vernant 1995, 12). Of course, *The Republic* makes scant provision for tragic spectacle in its vision of the ideal society. In contrast to the collective vision in which the community recognizes itself on stage, *The Republic* addresses what Plato viewed as the failure of tragedy to educate its audience. He turns away from the actual spectators in the *theatron* toward a more selective vision of an ideal audience; Plato's Socrates would confront us personally in order to inform "individual souls whose moral self-ordering is a prerequisite for political reconstitution" (Euben 1986, 9).

Plato's dialogues indeed share with tragedy the outward dramatic form of characters in debate. But the Platonic dialogue is also "theatre purged and purified of theatre's characteristic appeal to powerful emotion," according to Martha Nussbaum, so that the philosophic vision becomes a "pure crystalline theatre of the intellect" (1986, 133). The Platonic dialogue proceeds through an abstract, intellectual narrative to arrive at a philosophical account of things. But Nussbaum observes that tragedy acts as a warning against the dangers of any attempt to encompass the whole in purely intellectual terms. In contrast to the singular truth of Socrates' teaching, the "tragic *elenchos* does not present itself as part of an ongoing search for *the* correct account of anything" (134).

Attic tragedy relied on an emotional identification of spectator with the chorus and hero. This identification was effected primarily through interplay of the senses. "Tragedy's frequent use of synaesthetic imagery," Charles Segal comments, "and its explicit orchestration of visual and acoustic experience into moments of high drama call attention to this interconnection of the different senses" (1995, 213). These classical spectators were already attuned to the visual culture, fully capable of recognizing images and making sense of what was placed before their eyes. And the illustrative richness of the visible world was a significant, communal, and daily experience that encouraged a reciprocal development of the visual and dramatic arts. As Froma Zeitlin observes, this interpenetration of daily life, the decorative and plastic arts, and the visually evocative language of the dramatic stage all "share the requirement of an attentive gaze, a stylized and informed mode of viewing, which not only arouses spectators' affective responses but also engages their cognitive skills in learning how to recognize, evaluate, and interpret the visual codes of what they see" (1994, 140–41). So by combining familiar public iconography with dithyrambic odes sung to Dionysos, and borrowing from archaic religious rites and ritual dances, the tragic stage opened for the first time a public arena to confront the citizenry with their own history and so provoke them to question who they were.

The Aeschylean addition of the second actor to already familiar odes, religious rites, and visual symbols allowed the public to visualize itself "on stage." The chorus in particular, by virtue of being a crowd, allowed the spectators to recognize themselves not merely as a particular festival audience but also as part of a cohesive humanity.

Vision, as the ancients described it, was a luminous and projective activity involving object, light, and eye. Every significant element emanated a ray of vision, projecting outward and so commingling seeing and knowing as a common body of experience (Vernant 1995, 12–13). Applying the archaic experience of vision to the theatrical spectacle, one can begin to recognize that the spectator's outward gaze upon the stage is experienced and understood as a looking outside oneself and into the mirror of others as they face us. Vernant observes that "vision was only possible if there existed a total reciprocity between what was seen and the one who saw, conveying if not a complete identity between the two, then at least a very close kinship" (1995, 13).

Seated within the *theatron*, the spectator's vision would rove around, taking in the rows of fellow citizens and perhaps even the horizon beyond. So as they engaged the vision of others gazing back from the stage and audience, the personal vision of self came slowly into focus. The tragic spectacle unveiled the dramatic limits of personal and corporate identity and even of self-understanding: "Thus, what one was, one's face and soul, could be seen and known only by looking at the eye and the soul of another. Each person's identity was revealed through his relationship with others, through the intersecting of gazes and the exchanging of words" (Vernant 1995, 17).

Aristotle's inspection of rhetoric and tragedy was just such an attempt to visualize the power of persuasion (*peitho*) and the dramatic spectacle through intersecting gazes. Philosophy, from Aristotle's viewpoint, suggests how truth comes to light within these visual appearances when individuals come to know their place in the social context. A closer reading of the relevant texts is needed.

IV

The *Poetics* identifies six structural elements of tragedy: plot, character, thought, style (diction), lyric poetry (music), and spectacle. Aristotle describes and ranks these elements, turning to plot as the very life, soul, and first principle of tragedy. Plot is recognized as the greatest means of conveying emotional power. It is distinguished furthermore through its effect and then by the presence of two signature elements. Generalizing from the cases at hand, Aristotle observes that plots can be either simple or complex; the significant difference is that action in a complex plot turns on the intrinsic presence of either of two transformative elements: *peripeteia* (reversal) or *anagnorisis* (recognition).

Since an intrinsic transformation implies that some events should follow others (chapter 10), tragic plots must cohere and so attempt to weave together otherwise disparate elements. As Froma Zeitlin reminds us, Aristotle specifically emphasizes this elusive tragic unity, describing the tensions animating tragic plots as a "combination of *desis*, binding, and *lusis*, unbinding, denouement"; furthermore, Aristotle characterizes complex plots with the term *symploke*, bringing to mind a symbolic "interweaving, which describes the fabric, the texture of the play" (1990, 78–9). Tragic plots interweave a centripetal or cohesive force and a centrifugal or wandering, aimless tendency that nearly frustrates all attempts at stitching events together in a narrative line. But after all, Dionysos was the protean, feminine, and masked god who suffered repeated and symbolic dismemberment.

A reversal of fortune, as an intrinsic turn in the plot, is a "complete swing in the direction of the action" (Aristotle 1987, 11). And reversal foreshadows recognition. Aristotle then says that recognition, "as the very name shows, is a change from ignorance [*agnoia*] to knowledge, bringing the characters into either a close bond, or enmity, with one another, and concerning matters which bear on their prosperity or affliction" (11). As the very name shows, indeed, *anagnorisis*—recognition—is cognate with the archaic Greek for reading. So reading is an act of recognition, understood as the ability to decipher written marks by eye (see Havelock 1982 and Svenbro 1990). The verb for reading or picking up the narrative thread from the mute marks before our eyes, *anagignoskein*, resonates with Aristotle's term for recognizing the twists in the tragic plot line, *anagnorisis* (Segal 1995, 214).

We may thus infer that *anagnorisis*, the transformation from ignorance to knowledge, is related to literacy. Writing and reading now allow the detached theorist to derive abstraction from performance. Philosophic literacy then shows how issues come into focus before the mind's eye. When reading is likened to tragic recognition, however, philosophic literacy can seem a tragic misreading of an originally oral-performative phenomenon. Through analysis of the lively spectacle, the theorist also restricts the Dionysian energy within philosophic abstraction. In one sense this movement toward reading and away from the lively spectacle, however inevitable, is at least paradoxical if not itself tragic. Charles Segal observes that "the mentality of literacy and textual production seem almost indispensable to the structure of tragedy: the preplanned concentration of a complex action into a highly structured form, unfolding in a geometric, conventionalized, symbolic space" (1995, 213). The historical and psychological transformation that can be accounted for by this gradual but increasingly common practice of literacy is registered in Aristotle's recognition of the structural developments characterizing the tragic spectacle.

Aristotle's description of the function of rhetoric and of tragedy likewise involves significant metaphors related to *sight,* and *oversight,* and so conjoin the quest for a theoretical viewpoint with the issue of recognition. The architectonic metaphor of vision joins with the development of recognition as a political and psychological notion at crucial junctures in *On Rhetoric* and *The Poetics.*

I will begin with *On Rhetoric.* In Book I, on *"Pisteis"* or the means of persuasion, Aristotle describes how a previously aural and performative rhetoric now changes when read through the increasingly literate and detached viewpoint of philosophy. The famous opening definition of rhetoric that begins chapter two must be recalled: "Let rhetoric be [defined as] an ability, in each [particular] case, to see [*theoresai*] the available means of persuasion" (*On Rhetoric* 1.2.1.). The operative archaic word *theoresai* connotes "to be an observer of and to grasp the meaning of," as George Kennedy's insightful recent translation informs us (1991, 37). Furthermore, rhetoric is now placed before our theoretical gaze as an example of the genus Aristotle characterizes with the term *dynamis,* connoting an "ability, capacity, faculty." Rhetoric is not identified with a product (*ergon*) but rather with a process or capacity of visualization. This general ability to visualize the means available in each case is the function of no other art.

The definition of the nature and function of rhetoric links a linguistic and intellectual capacity, and this fateful crossroads of speech and thought is also the crucial issue where orality and literacy intersect. Aristotle's elaboration in chapter nineteen of *The Poetics* is worth citing: "Thought pertains to all those effects which must be produced by the spoken language; its functions are demonstration, refutation, the arousal of emotions such as pity, fear, anger, and such like, and arguing for the importance or unimportance of things" (1987, 53). Aristotle then refers us to *On Rhetoric* for a more complete analysis of the way thought and speech interrelate.

In Book III of *On Rhetoric,* Aristotle shows us in "Delivery, Style, and Arrangement" how to theorize *lexis*, or the narrative management of ideas. In chapters ten and eleven in particular, Aristotle discusses how various stylistic devices are cultivated by, and also become marks of, *urbanity* and thus how urbane civil speech has a particularly effective capacity for visualizing thought. The phrase here for visualization is *pro ommaton poiein*, literally meaning to "bring before the eyes." The urbane citizens of a *polis*, whose elegance and grace of expression naturally cultivate a pleasing relation with a hearer, can create knowledge almost effortlessly (1991, 10). Aristotle suggests this civilizing expression "should thus aim at three things: metaphor, antithesis, actualization [*energia*]" (1991, 11). The most energetic expressions are the most effective at "bringing before the eyes" or visualizing meaning for a hearer. A spectacular actualization moves thought by means of vivid stylistic speech (*ecphrasis*), just as energetic expression itself moves and lives and so characterizes a "well-directed mind" (1991, 11). Urbane speech is on target, directing the mentality of literacy by way of energetic expression, whereas orality wanders aimlessly and so misses the mark.

The difficulty with oral composition is that this earlier speech is so loosely constructed and amorphous that Aristotle's theoretical vision cannot contain it and so must overlook it. This produces a double bind: in the attempt to incorporate the unspeakable horrors and wrenching divisions of tragic consciousness within an urbane systematic theory, Aristotle sacrifices a core aspect of tragedy. Aristotle's insightful conjunction of linguistic and mental styles should have recognized these theoretical boundaries and interpretive limits yet did not. From Aristotle's viewpoint in retrospect, tragedy as a *literary genre* can be visualized as now moving from the rustic simplicity and directness of Aeschylean orality to the bookish and urbane sophistication of Euripidean literacy.

V

If to see is to know is to be, then what should the spectator make of what remains unseen but very real? For tragedy must not only visualize an inner-but-invisible self; it must also perform many backstage cultural negotiations for the Greeks. The audience of spectators seated in the *theatron* are placed ambiguously both with regard to the drama being staged for their pleasure and edification and to one another. In fifth century Athens, the south-facing dramatic theatre of Dionysos occupied a symbolic and didactic space in the city. Along a vertical or hierarchic axis, the *theatron* was situated midway between the public *agora,* or place of assembly at the base of the hill, and the sacred and spectacular temples crowning the Acropolis. This liminal locale suggested its symbolic function as mediator between public and private, personal and community identity (see Pozzi 1991). Thus, the spatial placement of the spectacle helped the assembled citizens visualize the conflicts embodied in a shift from a hierarchic to a more democratic politics as well as from *mythos* to *logos.*

The open-air theatre of Dionysos in Athens was a symbolic prototype so widely imitated that the dramatic spectacle extended to the very limits of the Greek-speaking world. In the original, a sweeping stepped-arch of ascending seats carved into a hillside overlooked both the distinctly bounded circle of the orchestra and the sea or horizon beyond. This view invited the audience to visualize the symbolic limits of recognition and to begin to sense the unseen but real force of the newly recognized mental horizon. Ruth Padel comments that the spatial syntax of the theatre embodied a "paradox of inside and outside, an open space making public that which was unseen, such as feelings, the past, the secrets of the 'house' " (1992, 9). By analogy, both the terrestrial and mental horizon can be understood as instances of the "boundary-situation" discussed by philosopher Karl Jaspers; because each age has its own psychic terrors and social tensions that threaten a productive life and well-ordered mind, tragedy—now as then—allows us to glimpse the horizon of meaning and thus confront the abyss or bounds of sense-making that enclose our lives (Sewall 1990).

Tragedy is framed through strategically situated boundaries, just as plots weave a hero's meaningful story out of otherwise mute gestures and inarticulate events. Tragedy takes us to the threshold of the visible and to the margins of the human for a glimpse into the abyss. Thus, we might speculate that these well-placed spectators could begin to sense the cosmic boundary that allows all living systems to recognize an *inner* self only by contrast with the *outer* contexts of life (see Bigger and Bigger 1982, 135). And the possibility of a meaningful *system* or coherent order of graphic signs is now recognized precisely because a horizon or limit to discursive activity is visualized. "Tragedy shows *us* the limits of meaning and knowledge," Timothy Reiss comments, "and *this* showing presupposes a human capacity for order" (1980, 11). Aristotle's incorporation of the tragic spectacle into the literate *Organon* can be read as placing recognition within the sphere of all such bio-theoretic, sense-making activities.

So the theatre staged and mediated conflicts along the horizon of life and death and on the vertical axis of the politics of social recognition. Yet tragedy also focused attention on the horizontal plane of cultural allegiances, especially the crucial interplay of center and periphery (see Davidson 1991). For the theatre of Dionysos occupied a liminal space overlooking the edge: with the center of the city, symbolized as the public hearth or common source of fire behind it, and the cold, vast, often empty land outside the walls enclosing the *polis* before it, the theatre dramatized how civilization itself is precariously balanced on the edge (see Pozzi 1995). This symbolic placement between order and chaos educated the citizens by allowing those assembled to visualize how civic culture (*paideia*) similarly radiates out from a cosmic center. We must be mindful that culture and community, as centripetal forms, are tragically dispersed by madness or chaos. The *theatron* offered spectators a dramatic presentation of the inevitable conflict of civilizing values and the barbaric world outside this charmed circle, recognized now as the Other, as *terra incognita* indeed (Zeitlin 1990).

VI

Recognition emerges as the philosophical issue at the core of Aristotle's influential reading of the tragic spectacle. The challenge for contemporary theorists is to incorporate recent work showing how the communicative modalities of orality and literacy affected Aristotle's reading of recognition. We must also recognize that one can understand tragedy by reading the *spectacle* phenomenologically. As Froma Zeitlin reminds us, *misreadings* are insightful precisely because they are ironic and inevitable: "Thus it is that irony is tragedy's characteristic trope; several levels of meaning operate at the same time. Characters speak without knowing what they say, and misreading is the typical and predictable response to the various cues that others give" (1990, 80).

The Poetics represents Aristotle's assimilation of the sheer terror and surprise of tragic recognition within the comforting civility of theory. Aristotle suggests the effects of reading or viewing tragedy are one and the same. Collapsing these communicative distinctions is a misreading insofar as Aristotle's silent reader as would-be-theorist of tragedy now begins to replace the dynamic and immediate confrontation of protagonist and spectator. The armchair theorist as silent reader necessarily excludes the subversive issues and recalcitrant elements not amenable to theory but powerfully present in the mind of the watching spectator. *On Rhetoric*, by emphasizing how the emotions can enable visualization, also shows how the tragic spectacle exercises its persuasive effect on those beginning to adopt the new form of literate thinking.

The *theatron* thus became the meeting place of differing levels of consciousness and modes of communication. It accentuated the distance between enactment and narration and between the world of the play and the world beyond the play, much as Timothy Reiss has observed: "Characterized by *distance*—both within discourse, which will now speak *of* something instead of simply *speaking*, and without discourse, since the spectator will have become an observer—this tragedy is the sign of some supposed knowledge, a knowledge already half consecrated" (1980, 8–9).

Tragic recognition, like the famous Delphic injunction to "know thyself," comes to mean, "know your mind by minding your place in the cosmic plot." *Anagnorisis* in the *tragic* sense cannot mean, as it will certainly tend to become after Descartes, "know thyself" as a solitary, abstract, and indubitable point in a cognitive plot. Descartes's famous *textual* formula "*cogito ergo sum*" dramatizes a new "enlightened" form of solitary and geometrical inference where the "I" or examined self becomes the sole and certain source of emotion and action, no longer half-hidden from human understanding. We must recognize that this Cartesian self is inferred from a wholly *textual* performance (see O'Neill 1989). Nor should classical *anagnorisis* be visualized as a palimpsest following Freud's assimilation of tragic recognition to a psychoanalytic viewpoint exposing layers or hidden chapters of the book-literate self.

Indeed, the essential enigma of the tragic spectacle was displaced by Aristotle's reading of recognition. This literate new key unlocked the previously mysterious problem of how the self plays into the social spectacle (see Veyne 1988, 29). The tragic spectator moves from ignorance toward knowledge as orality is recognized and distanced simultaneously with the arrival of the abstract *theoria* of the philosophers.

Works Cited

Aristotle. 1987. *The Poetics.* Trans. and commentary by Stephen Halliwell. Chapel Hill: University of North Carolina Press.
———. 1991. *On Rhetoric.* Trans. and notes by George A. Kennedy. New York: Oxford University Press.
Bigger, C. P., and C. A. H. Bigger. 1982. "Recognition in Biological Systems." In *Philosophy and Archaic Experience,* ed. John Sallis, 122–49. Pittsburgh: Duquesne University Press.
Cave, Terence. 1990. *Recognitions: A Study in Poetics.* Oxford: Clarendon Press.
Davidson, Jean M. 1991. "Myth and the Periphery." In *Myth and the Polis,* ed. Dora C. Pozzi and John M. Wickersham, 49–63. Ithaca: Cornell University Press.
Euben, J. Peter, ed. 1986. *Greek Tragedy and Political Theory.* Berkeley: University of California Press.

Grassi, Ernesto. 1980. *Rhetoric as Philosophy: The Humanist Tradition*. University Park: Pennsylvania State University Press.

Gellrich, Michelle. 1988. *Tragedy and Theory: The Problem of Conflict since Aristotle*. Princeton: Princeton University Press.

Gomperz, Theodor. 1901. *Greek Thinkers: A History of Ancient Philosophy*. Trans. Laurie Magnus. London: John Murray.

Gouldner, Alvin. 1971. *Enter Plato: Classical Greece and the Origins of Social Theory, Part II*. New York: Harper & Row.

Havelock, Eric. 1982. *The Literate Revolution in Greece and Its Cultural Consequences*. Princeton: Princeton University Press.

Nussbaum, Martha. 1986. *The Fragility of Goodness*. New York: Cambridge University Press.

Padel, Ruth. 1990. "Making Space Speak." In *Nothing to Do with Dionysos? Athenian Drama in Its Social Context*, ed. John J. Winkler and Froma I. Zeitlin, 336–65. Princeton: Princeton University Press.

———. 1992. *In and Out of the Mind: Greek Images of the Tragic Self*. Princeton: Princeton University Press.

Pozzi, Dora C. 1991. "The Polis in Crisis." In *Myth and the Polis*, ed. Dora C. Pozzi and John M. Wickersham, 126–63. Ithaca: Cornell University Press.

Reiss, Timothy. 1980. *Tragedy and Truth: Studies in the Development of a Renaissance and Neoclassical Discourse*. New Haven: Yale University Press.

Sallis, John. 1986. *Being and Logos: The Way of Platonic Dialogue*. Atlantic Highlands: Humanities Press.

Segal, Charles. 1986. *Interpreting Greek Tragedy: Myth, Poetry, Text*. Ithaca: Cornell University Press.

———. 1995. "Spectator and Listener." In *The Greeks*, ed. Jean-Pierre Vernant, 184–217. Ithaca: Cornell University Press.

Sewall, Richard. 1990. *The Vision of Tragedy: Tragic Themes in Literature from the Book of Job to O'Neill and Miller*. New York: Paragon House.

Svenbro, Jesper. 1990. "The 'Interior' Voice: On the Invention of Silent Reading." In *Nothing to Do with Dionysos? Athenian Drama in Its Social Context*, ed. John J. Winkler and Froma I. Zeitlin, 366–84. Princeton: Princeton University Press.

Vernant, Jean-Pierre. 1982. *The Origins of Greek Thought*. Ithaca: Cornell University Press.

———, ed. 1995. *The Greeks*. Trans. Charles Lambert and Teresa Lavender Fagen. Chicago: University of Chicago Press.

Vernant, Jean-Pierre, and Pierre Vidal-Naquet. 1988. *Myth and Tragedy in Ancient Greece*. Trans. Janet Lloyd. New York: Zone Books.

Veyne, Paul. 1988. *Did the Greeks Believe Their Myths? An Essay on the Constitutive Imagination*. Trans. Paula Wissing. Chicago: University of Chicago Press.

Wilshire, Bruce. 1991. *Role Playing and Identity: The Limits of Theatre as Metaphor*. Bloomington: Indiana University Press.

Zeitlin, Froma I. 1990. "Playing the Other: Theater, Theatricality, and the

Feminine in Greek Drama." In *Nothing to Do with Dionysos? Athenian Drama in Its Social Context,* ed. John J. Winkler and Froma I. Zeitlin, 63–96. Princeton: Princeton University Press.

———. 1994. "The Artful Eye: Vision, *Ecphrasis* and Spectacle in Euripidean Theatre." In *Art and Text in Ancient Greek Culture,* ed. Simon Goldhill and Robin Osborne, 138–96. Cambridge: Cambridge University Press.

Exile and the Kingdom

Reason as Nightmare in the Aeschylean Vision

John Arthos

I

*I*N HIS STUDY of Greek tragedy, Rush Rehm differentiates between modern and ancient notions of ritual. Whereas today we
distinguish rituals that entail an act of belief from those that entail a
suspension of disbelief, in ancient Athens ritual and belief coexisted as
points on "a continuum of performance rather than as opposed atti-
tudes to the world. . . . The areas of politics, law, religion, athletics, festivals, music, and poetry shared with the theatre an essentially public
and performative nature, so much so that one form of cultural expression merged easily with another (1992, 3). This blurring of institu-
tional boundaries is attributable to the indistinctness of the categories
of law, religion, and philosophy in the discourse of the Greek polis. The
claims of the individual against larger societal claims or against the
claims of tradition were new, struggling out of forms of discourse
shaped in earlier times. New thinking had not yet evolved new institutions reflecting these distinctions.

In Aeschylus's *The Suppliants,* the vocabulary of religious and moral
concerns merges with the language of the court. *Warrants, charges, in-
junctions, arraignments, claimants, payments, judgments* are English words
used to translate Greek concepts that had a wider range. Because democratic law at this moment was anything but clear and fully formed—
emerging slowly from a welter of myth, religion, custom, and rule—its
language was supple, protean, and richly ambiguous.[1] Aeschylus exploits
this suppleness in Greek vocabulary to develop his central enigmas.

---

[1]Vernant and Vidal-Naquet write substantially about the nexus of society, law, and art
in their groundbreaking work, *Myth and Tragedy in Ancient Greece:* "The tragic poets
make use of this legal vocabulary, deliberately exploiting its ambiguities, its fluctuations,

A society that had begun to examine its own assumptions about right and wrong through an *agon* of reason, custom, and authority naturally allowed the deeper dimensions of moral imagination to invade the legal and political arena. The institution of the festival drama found its public voice in working out the implications of these political developments. My contention is that *The Suppliants* dramatized for the Athenian audience a disquieting development that confronted their society: the frightening burden of reason and choice necessitated by the abandonment of unquestioned authority.

II

The action of the play centers on a question of asylum. The fifty daughters of Danaus flee Egypt to avoid their pursuing cousins, the sons of Aegyptus, who intend to force a marriage claim. The daughters seek protection in Argos, the homeland of Io, from whom they claim descent. The king of Argos hears their plea, confers with his subjects, and grants asylum. The sons of Aegyptus arrive, make their claim, and are rebuffed.[2] As numerous scholars have made clear, the Egyptian men's claim for marriage is legitimate under the laws of patrimony, but the Danaids' rebellion grows from deep-seated incest taboo. Attic law encouraged the family to protect estate property through marriage, and because Danaus had no male heir, the cousins would have felt positive duty to secure the estate through marriage. Exogamy is a tricky matter in ancient Greece because it is not based strictly on consanguinity (Durkheim 1963, 63–69). The king asks the Danaids why they flee their cousins:

KING: By reason of hatred? Or do you speak of unlawfulness?

CHORUS: Who would purchase their lords from among their kin?

KING: Tis thus that families have their power enhanced.

CHORUS: Aye, tis easy then, if things go ill, to put away a wife.
(Aeschylus 1963, ll. 336–39)

---

and its incompleteness. We find an imprecision in the terms used, shifts of meaning, incoherences and contradictions" (47).

[2] *The Suppliants* is thought to be the first of a trilogy. Fragments of the lost *Egyptians* and *Danaids*, the second and third plays respectively, suggest that the women are captured by the Egyptians and defend their virginity by murdering their captors. One of the women breaks ranks and marries her lover. She is tried for her defection but in the end wins her defense before the court of Aphrodite (Murray 1959, 11).

Incest is suggested, rebuffed, and discarded in this passage. The nature of this exchange suggests that the taboo exists but on some more tenuous and submerged level of contested moral terrain (see Gilbert Murray 1959, 15, and Burian 1991, xxiii). The claim of property rights is asserted and challenged in turn by the Danaids but this time from a different angle. If a woman is to be taken at will without her consent, she will just as easily be killed when she becomes an inconvenience. The Danaids try to subvert the property argument by claiming *they* cannot be treated as property. They are not chattel. They wish to be regarded as fully human, with the right to accept or reject a proposal of marriage. The assertion of human and individual rights, if given its due, will complicate things enormously.

The drama is not the reenactment of a political debate in the marketplace. Its role is to reveal the wider implications of such decisions. *The Suppliants* does this by opening the ties of history to myth and poetic imagery to reason. The turn to reason entails no Enlightenment optimism, no progression towards clarity and certainty, but a vertiginous falling into a world of new dangers.

The ancestry of the participants in the drama is crucial to the meanings of the play. Io, the Argive priestess of Hera, was courted by Zeus. Hera, incensed by this betrayal, drove Io from her home, turned her into a heifer to wander the earth tortured unremittingly by a gadfly. Io ultimately arrived in Egypt, where Zeus returned her to human form and blessed her with a son, Epaphus, whose lineage reaches to the children of Danaus and Aegyptus (to whom the suppliant women trace their line). Io, a priestess of Hera, is betrayed by the lust of Zeus. The Danaids flee for sanctuary to Argos, claiming kinship with Io, and prostrate themselves before Zeus, the god of suppliants. This fateful irony constitutes the subtext of the play. Each time the daughters of Danaus invoke Zeus (protector/seducer) for mercy, the contradictions resonate. Each of the many times[3] the suppliants recount the story of Io, Zeus's compromised position is placed in relief.

The moral irony of the circumstance is the texture of the Aeschylean problem, the ground from which he mines his effects. In *The Suppliants,* the irony is so carefully masked that it operates at an almost subliminal level. The protector/seducer conflict is insistent but submerged, working off a relationship of background to foreground. Robert Murray shows that Zeus's duplicity is marked so gently that it has escaped most

---

[3]The Zeus/Io story is mentioned eight times explicitly over the course of the drama, and indirectly many more.

critics (Murray 1958, 58). The Danaids regard Zeus's intervention to end Io's torment as her salvation, as the name of the child born to her, Epaphus, meaning divine caress or touching of the god, would emphasize. But this intervention is the consummation of Zeus's intentions from the beginning. The description of the act of procreation substitutes the word for the divine breath (*ephaptor*) in the last instance for a word (*rousion*) that carries a suggestion of violence or coercion (ll. 313–15). Similarly, the word *kratos* is used throughout the play to refer to the absolute power of the king and of divine authority, but at the very end (1068) the same word is used to describe the suppliants' victory when they have gained their freedom from the tyranny of their cousins by the will of the people of Argos. The elasticity of the word *kratos* (power/victory) is used to signal the profound movement of power away from absolute patriarchy.

The tensions operating within the play work to subvert its ostensible purposes. In spite of the clear sympathies of the principals towards the women, the sons of Aegyptus have legal precedent on their side. The suppliants turn to *Zeus* for protection from male domination. The king of Argos proclaims himself lord and ruler of his land, bragging that it is only "the boundary of the liquid sea" that restrains his realm, yet when foreign women ask him for sanctuary, he must consult his people and yield to their decision. These tensions gather and coalesce. They are not simply issues to be sorted out; they are the knotted fabric of human experience, and the play weaves its dread out of these multiple contradictions.

At the center of the play is the image of nightmare. Hera devised a torture for Io that was, like Prometheus's torture, exquisite, an unremitting pain that exacerbated the suffering of exile (see Murray 1958, 56). While Io was reminded every moment of her life that she was estranged from everything familiar and comforting, she was literally made strange by her transformation. A grotesque image, like Yeats's slouching beast, finds eerie reflection in the fate of the suppliants: "Mortals who in those days were indwellers of the land, shook with terror at the sight of a fearsome being half-human, part of the race of kine and part of woman; awestruck at the monstrous thing" (Aeschylus 565).

Aeschylus did not need to make explicit this image of deformity, and it foregrounds the most nightmarish aspect of the Io story. The play is woven out of the images of wretched and cruel beasts, of carrion and shameless dogs, especially of the beasts of prey at that moment when they have ensnared their quarry. The humiliation and helplessness of the goaded heifer, however, is the most insistent image, recalling us to the nightmare of this special exile.

III

Ostracism was a devastating political act in ancient Greece. Following Stoessl, Anthony Podlecki develops the theory that Aeschylus wrote *The Suppliants* in response to the ostracism of Themistocles, a political event that occurred shortly before current estimates of the date of the play (Podlecki 1966, 52). Themistocles was condemned for collaborating to betray Hellas to Xerxes; he was ostracized and fled to avoid prosecution. He sought asylum in Argos but then fled even Argos to escape further pursuit. Podlecki cites these parallel events as proof of Aeschylus's political intentions for *The Suppliants* (Podlecki 1966, 53). The close conceptual alignment of ostracism, exile, and asylum binds together the stories of Io, the Danaids, and Themistocles to point to the extraordinary value Athenians placed on citizenship.

The play may be addressing, more abstractly, the profound sense of dislocation Athenians felt as they moved away from the absolute authority of kings and gods to the terrible responsibility of their own reason. The suppliants remind the king that he is "a lord subject to no judge" (375). The king, however, instead of ruling by the established claim of authority, deliberates with his people about relative claims. As he sets out to meet with his citizens in assembly he hesitates from fright before his task: "Surely you cannot think there is no need of salutary counsel?" He compares such an act to that of a diver who must "descend into the depths" (410), and the decision, either way, "is a sea of ruin, fathomless and impassable, that I have launched upon, and nowhere is there a haven from distress" (470). The parallel between the king and the suppliants is unavoidable—relinquishing absolute authority on the one hand, denying patriarchal rule on the other. In either case there is no haven.

What this play reveals about the horizons of the Athenian vision is quite stunning. The frightening price for self-reliance, for turning to reason and away from authority, is prefigured in (and then read back into) Greek mythology. Prometheus, Daedalus, Odysseus, all open Pandora's box. The penalty for turning away from unquestioned authority is torture, deformity, exile, death.[4] The suppliant women defy the laws

---

[4] The irony is that the ascendancy of reason here is the precise inverse of the Enlightenment approach to rationalism. Whereas Descartes sought in the rational reduction progress towards distinctness and clarity, for the ancient Greeks that which was distinct and clear was divine knowledge, and what resided in the realm of human knowledge was conjecture and uncertainty. Aeschylus is in this sense closer to Adorno and Horkheimer than Descartes or Habermas.

of patrimony and choose their fate; a king trembles at the defiance of custom. The consequences of just this kind of overreaching inform the tragic material. The Athenian demos was venturing into these deep waters, abandoning the safety of tradition, questioning authority, and divesting power. The reaction later in the fifth century to the ascendance of Greek rationalism is well documented.[5] Disbelief in the supernatural was made an indictable offense in the last third of the fifth century: heresy trials became common and banishment resulted frequently. Protagoras's books were collected and burned, and he was pursued in flight to his death; hysteria and persecution followed the mutilation of the Hermae; Aristophanes burns down the Thinking Shop. The unease expressed in Aeschylean imagery was, it turns out, prophetic.

The irresolution and torn consciousness, tension and ambivalence of the early fifth century were concomitant with the loosening of traditional assurance. This unbinding occasioned a fear of being launched out to sea, "a sea of ruin, fathomless and impassable" (470). The images of the play are images that must have struck home because a society that has turned its back on the certainties of tradition is itself in a sense in exile. It has exposed itself and cut its ties. It is in danger of wandering, like Io, an alien, despised and reduced, revealed and humiliated in the error of its choice. At the center of the play is nightmare, a monstrous thing, half human, half beast, a defilement. Tortured by its public exposure, the creature wishes only to flee to "some dark hiding-place, to vanish like black smoke . . . quite out of sight like viewless dust, and dissolve into nothingness" (780).

The power of this tragedy lies in its capacity to evoke the primal fear embodied by the fleeing suppliant women. Destitute in an alien land and racked by the panic of pursuit, they are outcasts from law, defenseless and exposed. Exile haunts the Greek mind, and this play works the theme through all of its registers. Mythic parallel, dramatic enactment, choral lyric, and intricate imagery coalesce to suggest the terror of isolation and ruin as the condition of humanity. Aeschylus's vision is of the terror that opens up in the moment of ultimate flight. In light of our contemporary turning from enlightenment faith to the dislocations of the irrational, this frightened Aeschylean descent into reason and choice provides a very different view of the penalties attendant on a rational world.

---

[5]See, for example, E. R. Dodds, *The Greeks and the Irrational.* (186–89).

Works Cited

Aeschylus. 1963. *The Suppliants*. Trans. Herbert Weir Smyth. Cambridge: Harvard University Press.

Burian, Peter. 1991. Introduction to *The Suppliants*. Princeton: Princeton University Press.

Dodds, E. R. 1951. *The Greeks and the Irrational*. Berkeley: University of California Press.

Durkheim, Emile. 1963. *Incest: The Nature and Origin of the Taboo*. Trans. Albert Ellis. New York: Lyle Stuart.

Hogan, James C. 1984. *A Commentary on the Complete Greek Tragedies: Aeschylus*. Chicago: University of Chicago Press.

Horkheimer, Max, and Theodor W. Adorno. 1972. *Dialectic of Enlightenment*. Trans. John Cumming. New York: Seabury Press.

Lattimore, Richmond. 1964. *Story Patterns in Greek Tragedy*. Ann Arbor: University of Michigan Press.

Lembke, Janet. 1975. Introduction to *The Suppliants*. New York: Oxford University Press.

Murray, Gilbert. 1959. Introduction to *The Suppliants*. London: George Allen and Unwin.

Murray, Robert, Jr. 1958. *The Motif of Io in Aeschylus' Suppliants*. Princeton: Princeton University Press.

Podlecki, Anthony J. 1966. *The Political Background of Aeschylean Tragedy*. Ann Arbor: University of Michigan Press.

Rehm, Rush. 1992. *Greek Tragic Theatre*. London: Rutledge.

Ridgeway, William. 1966. *The Origin of Tragedy*. New York: Benjamin Blom.

Rose, H. J. 1957. *A Commentary on the Surviving Plays of Aeschylus*. Amsterdam: N.V. Noord-Hollandsche Uitgevers Maatschappij.

Snell, Bruno. 1960. *The Discovery of the Mind: The Greek Origins of European Thought*. New York: Harper and Row.

Stoessl, Franz. 1988. *Der Prometheus des Aischylos als Geistesgeschichtliches und Theatergeschichtliches Phänomen*. Stuttgart: Franz Steiner.

Tucker, T. G. 1889. Critical Notes to *The Suppliants*. London: Macmillan and Co.

Vernant, Jean-Pierre, and Vidal-Naquet, Pierre. 1988. *Myth and Tragedy in Ancient Greece*. New York: Zone Books.

Winkler, John J., and Froma I. Zeitlin, eds. 1990. *Nothing to Do with Dionysos? Athenian Drama in Its Social Context*. Princeton: Princeton University Press.

Epideictic Pastoral

Rhetorical Tensions in the
Staging of Torquato Tasso's *Aminta*

Maria Galli Stampino

*D*URING THE PAST few decades, the culture of the Renaissance has elicited a flurry of reinterpretations and "re-readings," many of which derived their tools from approaches traditionally excluded or at least marginalized from the exploration and interpretation of this particular time period. The fields of Renaissance theatre and performance have not lagged behind. The present work, however, originates from the awareness that little attention has been devoted to classical rhetoric in contemporary efforts to recreate and evaluate Renaissance literary, theatrical, and in general cultural expressions. An impetus in this direction derives from a seminal article published by Brian Vickers in 1983 forcefully asserting the need for scholars to realize the relevance of the classical rhetorical tradition to the literature of the past. More important for theatre scholars, he goes on to declare that "not only works of literature but modes of reading literature were shaped by rhetoric, and this in ways which may surprise us" (1983, 498). In other words, during the Renaissance the fruition as well as the production of literature were under the sway of classical rhetoric.

Although his article centers around how "the Renaissance *reader* approached his *books*" (1983, 499; emphases added), I would like to focus on how the stage, and in particular pastoral drama, can be grasped within the frame of rhetoric. My attempt is better described as "reconstruction" than as "interpretation" or "understanding." Indeed, I be-lieve that for too long the field of performance studies (especially within the Italian tradition) has been influenced by literary methodologies aimed at reading and interpreting texts. In the case of the theatre, how-ever, the objects under scrutiny are much more complex than are writ-ten texts; therefore, I contend that a purely hermeneutic strategy proves utterly inadequate. This is why I tend toward a "reconstruction" of texts-based events and also why I am convinced that classical rhetoric proves to be an invaluable tool.[1]

I will restrict the following remarks to one particular text-based event, the Italian pastoral play *Aminta,* written by Torquato Tasso pre-sumably at Ferrara in 1573. There are three fundamental sets of rea-sons for this choice. First, *Aminta* was a highly significant text for the Italian and the European Renaissance, spawning a host of similar plays that were staged well into the eighteenth century.[2] If a rhetorical ap-proach proves to clarify and enhance our understanding in this instance, the relevance of such an approach to other works will be decisively cor-roborated. Second, Tasso's pastoral was instantly famous, especially in courtly circles. Hence, there are plenty of extant documents pertaining to both its written text and its performances. Therefore, the proposed reconstructive task is somewhat eased. Last, *Aminta* was integrated in the canon of Italian literature and theatre from a very early date after its first performance, and consequently critical assessments are particu-larly abundant. Hence, it is easy to utilize such secondary literature to define the current endeavor and to understand to what extent this text-based event has been miscast until now.

Two additional elements deserve mention here, as they justify the

---

[1]Vickers, too, asserts that scholars of the Renaissance are "concern[ed] with recon-structing the past," an endeavor that transforms them into "an anomaly, or at best a minority, in a world overwhelmingly concerned with the present" (1983, 497). Although this is still largely the case, the prodigious technological developments of the last five to ten years have had the beneficial effect of stirring a debate about how to keep and transmit the present and the past to the future, in literature, the visual arts, and the realm of the performative. Witness to this trend is the conference "Seeing/Saving Performance," orga-nized by the Performance Studies division at the Speech Communication Association con-vention of 1995.

[2]According to Angelo Ingegneri, one of the most famous "directors" of the period, the pastoral as a genre must be credited with saving the practice of theatrical entertainment: "If pastorals did not exist, we could say that we would have lost the usage of the stage. Consequently the main goal of playwrights (that is, having their works staged) would have become desperate, and with time passing, we would not have found a poet willing to compose even a few lines for the stage" ([1598] 1974, 275; translation mine).

emphasis on *Aminta* and reinforce the relevance of the proposed approach. The pastoral as a genre is particularly well suited for understanding the pervasive presence of rhetoric in Renaissance literature.
The pastoral—due to its setting, its plot, and its characters' relations—
tends to be highly idealized. Therefore, it easily becomes a forum for
rhetorical exhortations. Moreover, Tasso wrote for the court, and a great
number of *Aminta* stagings took place in the context of courtly entertainment. Therefore, the play implies a specific sort of audience, one
comprising the ruler and his courtiers. Such an audience served as a
perfect target for the exhortation of a rhetorical performance. Additionally, the circumstances of such courtly stagings were festive; performances took place during special times when the court celebrated an
event that required some amount of highlighting. Consequently, these
stagings take on additional meaning, as the *festa* is always marked by a
specific teleology. In Cruciani and Seragnoli's words, "whether small or
large, religious or private, the festivity constitutes a non-everyday-like
time structure. It is not simply entertainment or distraction; indeed, it
always displays its social and cultural meaning" (1987, 17; translation
mine).

Given how little attention has been devoted to rhetoric in literary
circles, it is hardly surprising that only one critic has linked *Aminta*
(albeit indirectly) with the effects it had on its audience. Writing in
1980, Dante Della Terza asserts that this pastoral play "aims, first and
foremost, to persuade and edify an audience who is at the same time
from Ferrara and from the court" (51; translation mine). By bringing
up the "persuasion" and "edification" of the implied audience, Della
Terza hints that *Aminta* can be cast in the light of epideictic rhetoric,
one of the three branches described by Aristotle. For the latter, "the
elements of an epideictic speech are praise and blame" projected on
"the present, for everyone praises or blames with regard to existing conditions, though a speaker often adds to his resources with reminiscences
from the past and conjectures about the future" (1960, 17–18). Della
Terza has the merit of being the only scholar to point out these fundamental traits. However, his important reference to epideictic rhetoric
shows the limited scope he attributes to it: a local audience, particularly
the one at the Ferrara court, where Tasso wrote his pastoral, but which
might never have seen *Aminta* performed.[3] Della Terza's contribution

---

[3]The issue of whether *Aminta* was performed in Ferrara in 1573, soon after its composition, is still highly controversial. The hypothesis of a *premiere* in July of that year was
first put forth by Angelo Solerti in his biography of Tasso (on the basis of circumstantial

is crucial and needs to be expanded because *Aminta* was surprisingly popular in courts all over Italy for a considerable number of years, as well as on the makeshift stages of *commedia dell'arte* troupes.

The courtly setting of many *Aminta* performances provides a privileged point of departure for their reconstruction along epideictic lines. Late Renaissance courts throughout Europe were given to continuous, and self-conscious, productions representing themselves and their relations. For example, Frank Whigham has argued that in Elizabethan England, "public life at court had come under a new and rhetorical imperative of performance. *Esse sequitur operare:* identity was to be derived from behavior. Ruling-class status, desired and performed alike, had become not a matter of being but of doing, and so of *showing*" (1983, 625). At court, in England as well as in post-Tridentine Catholic countries like Italy, France, and Spain, people found themselves in the midst of a continual representation of their selves and their social place and position: "Identity comes close to becoming a pure commodity generated (however self-consciously) for conversational consumption" (631). In short, "the ideal courtier is never offstage" (634) because he is under the constant gaze of his fellow noblemen (and, more rarely, women) as well as of his underlings and the commoners (632). Life at court hence *is* epideictic.[4]

This epideictic spirit was especially heightened on specific occasions such as courtly entertainments, particularly theatrical performances. Clearly, as courtly events these performances were public, although attendance was restricted. Alain Godard, for example, has examined the supposed *premiere* of *Aminta* and, more generally, the difference between pastoral performances and tournaments at the Ferrara court during the 1560s and 1570s. He maintains that pastoral plays were much less important on the public level than the highly choreographed chivalric tournaments often performed there:

> The great chivalric tournament is also a popular festival, or to be more precise, a festival during which the duke and the noblemen, adorned with all the wizardry of a show, let themselves be seen by a popular audience. It is the occasion for an exceptional affirmation of the hegemonic voca-

---

evidence alone) (1895, 1: 181–85), and subsequently espoused by most critics. Only recently has some debate begun about the plausibility of such an interpretation: see in particular Cruciani 1985.

[4]E. R. Curtius points out that Aristotle's third rhetorical *genus* is termed either epideictic or panegyrical; "the term *epídeixis* goes back to its aspect of display, the term *panegurikós* to the outward occasion" (1953, 69 n. 15).

tion of the nobility and of the ruler's dynasty. All the components and all the functions of the court are presented in the tournament theater, in an emblematic synthesis. On the contrary, with pastoral stagings, the court's political and hegemonic responsibilities fade; the court is no longer above all the center of power and the point of convergence of the social structure. Rather, it is the dwelling place of a learned, privileged elite, which is held together, in spite of the differences in rank, by the same lifestyle, and which shares common predilections and aspirations. (1977, 200–202; translation mine)

Although Godard builds an impressive argument, he fails to consider that the organizers of pastoral entertainment were closely linked to the court and that most performances took place in ducal buildings or in villas belonging to other courtiers. It is undeniable, therefore, that although restricted to a highly selected audience, such pastoral performances were far from private. Rather, they fell within the public arena, in one of the senses delineated by Jürgen Habermas: "We call events and occasions 'public' when they are open to all, in contrast to closed or exclusive affairs—as when we speak of public places or public houses. But as in the expression 'public building,' the term need not refer to general accessibility; the building does not even have to be open to public traffic. 'Public buildings' simply house state institutions and as such are 'public' " (1989, 1–2). Therefore, performances of *Aminta* (indeed, courtly performances of any theatrical text) are simultaneously cloistered and public.[5] They fall in a gray zone between public relevance and private entertainment. Precisely because of their unique status, however, pastoral plays particularly profit from a rhetorical analysis according to the categories of the epideictic. As public performances they constitute one of the tools in the ruler's hands for influencing the public at large; as restricted, they tend to embody ideals in which the court could recognize itself.

Due to its patent lack of reference to everyday existence, even in the pampered lives of the courtiers, the pastoral is a genre at the convergence between Neoplatonic trends and Aristotelian rules. Because of Aristotle's wording of the preferred topic for an epideictic speech,

---

[5]One of the most obvious (and pernicious) consequences of Solerti's reconstruction of the events of *Aminta*'s opening is the tendency to place it in a solitary place, a *locus amœnus* where the duke and his courtiers would retire precisely to forget the worries of the palace. Consequently, the public relevance of such an event goes mostly unrecognized, while the tendency prevails to read the pastoral in escapist terms.

"much of Renaissance literature . . . suffers from being divided into . . . sharply opposed binary categories. Virtue or vice, praise or blame, are instantly recognizable, since the whole of human experience is polarized into these extremes" (Vickers 1983, 507). Such a stance fits very well indeed with the Neoplatonic ideals permeating the Renaissance and becomes particularly concrete in the genre of the pastoral. Yet the Aristotelian debt is obvious in the practical turn that literature acquires in this period. Virtually no text from any genre is devoid of the goal of showing the path to (or examples of) virtue to its audience.[6] Theatre is especially susceptible to the same moralizing and didactic concerns, as is evident in the words of two theatre practitioners and authors of the period. Writing presumably in the 1560s, Leone de' Sommi defines a play as "nothing but the imitation or exemplary portrait of human life, in which vices must be denounced (so as to flee them) and virtues exposed (so as to imitate them)" ([1560?] 1968, 12; translation mine). Epideixis is not explicitly mentioned, but it constitutes a necessary implication of de' Sommi's definition. At the end of the century, in 1598, Angelo Ingegneri more specifically links the need of a play to adhere to the truth ("verisimilitude") with the effects that it elicits from its audience: "the closer what is uttered on stage is to reality, the more effective it is in moving or affecting" the audience ([1598] 1974, 277; translation mine). The proposed epideictic approach thus offers the added advantage of avoiding the imposition of subsequent categories to the reconstruction of late Renaissance events.

Historically, too, epideictic rhetoric played a crucial role. At the time that the pastoral flourished (the last quarter of the sixteenth century and the first half of the seventeenth), the production of literary and theatrical texts became progressively more subject to strict rules. The monarchies of France, Spain, and England were concentrating in their hands the lands and powers previously divided among several noble families (a process variously known as "creation of the modern state" or "absolutism"). Catholic areas (including Italy, where no single ruling family prevailed yet) were also coping with the decrees of the Council of Trent (1545–1563), which prescribed minutely the topics that were

---

[6]Vickers asserts that "rhetoric and poetics are thus instrumental faculties which the citizen employs for action, namely, to make his fellow citizens good" (1983, 509). This wording reflects an idealized image of early Renaissance city-states that recent historiography has largely debunked. As I will try to show, Vickers's assertion also clashes with the historical frame of the *Aminta* performances under scrutiny here.

acceptable (and those recommended) in literature and even in the visual arts.[7] Because the other two Aristotelian rhetorical forms (the deliberative and the forensic) had lost their import in such a centralized society, and because of the "confident belief in the power of literature to reach its audience and change it" (Vickers 1983, 510), rhetorically shaped literature had become both a rare tool to counsel the ruler and an important means of influence over peers and subjects. It would be simplistic, therefore, to see pastoral plays as solely a means to impose an interpretation or an alternative view of reality on commoners and courtiers alike. The tension created by court-staged pastorals ran both ways, making their impact more cogent.

If the preceding assertions clash with our aesthetic concepts, it is because our views of literature (and also of theatre) have changed dramatically in the intervening years. One of the most difficult stumbling blocks for a twentieth-century scholar examining the theatre of the Renaissance is that we cannot be sure, in many cases, of the referentiality of the bodies on the stage—that is, if they were perceived as bodies of actors and actresses possessed with separate identities and referring while in character to something existing elsewhere.[8] More than likely, in the early period of the popularity of the pastoral, the line between characters, bodies, and performers was blurry at best. It is therefore possible to assert that on one more important count *Aminta* was an epideictic text: its characters, usually criticized as wooden,[9] are not

---

[7]The much dreaded institution of the *Index librorum prohibitorum* was greatly reinforced by the decrees of the Council, and a similar list of inappropriate and indecent images did not come into existence solely because of a series of circumstances, including the early death of Cardinal Giovanni Paleotti of Bologna, one of its most vehement proponents and supporters. On these events and their ideological background see Prodi 1965, particularly 142–47.

[8]Solerti's hypothesis regarding the opening of *Aminta* is largely based on the ability, on the part of the audience, to separate the identity of the performers (supposedly the famed *commedia dell'arte* troupe of the Gelosi) both from the characters embodied on stage and from the oblique references to people at court that Tasso supposedly interspersed throughout the play. These elements reinforce the implausibility of Solerti's hypothesis because it appears to have been clearly influenced by ulterior motives and by subsequent categories. Indeed in de' Sommi's third dialogue, when the conversation turns to the performers' costumes and masks, Veridico ("he who tells the truth") asserts that "if the spectator recognizes the player, then the sweet illusion partially disappears that should enthrall the audience: the latter should believe as much as possible that the events of each performance take place in reality" ([1560?] 1968, 50; translation mine).

[9]According to Mario Fubini, for example, we should talk "of silhouettes, and stylized ones at that, rather than of characters, for Silvia, Aminta, Dafne and Tirsi" (1971, 211; translation mine). Eugenio Donadoni goes further: "Tasso feels no joy in looking into the

meant to reproduce human beings (whether fictional or real); rather, they are intended as embodiments of ideas and virtues: "The Renaissance reader was accustomed, in theory at least, to seeing each character not as a complex, autonomous personality but as an illustration of a virtue. . . . Secondly, . . . the Renaissance reader saw only the virtue represented in the character [and] looked through him, as if using an X-ray, to the moral quality and ignored other, less essential aspects of his or her behavior" (Vickers 1983, 522).

In sum, what constitutes a weakness for a twentieth-century reader or theatregoer was indeed an advantage for a Renaissance viewer.[10] Therefore, *Aminta* falls in the same category as the earlier treatises aimed at educating the perfect courtier (such as Baldassar Castiglione's *The Courtier*, written in 1526). Because of its public nature as staged entertainment, its scope exceeds the boundaries of the court and enters the public arena at large. Certainly different social and political conditions required new examples to be set forth for the courtiers, and, in my opinion, this need accounts for the fact that tracts and printed dialogues were being replaced by theatrical performances aiming at instructing while entertaining. It is a recognition of the effectiveness of the theatre at the end of the Renaissance and into the Baroque period because of its ability to reach larger audiences (including the illiterates) and its clarity in giving life to moral and behavioral examples. It also highlights the multifaceted ability of these performers, who exploited skills and resources from different sources (religious preaching as well as classical rhetorical tenets inculcated into any pupil: see Cruciani and Seragnoli 1987, 18) in order to entertain and sway their audience.[11]

---

reality and the mystery of the human psyche. There is no crisis in the characters. Each one of them is at the end the same as at the beginning" (1952, 110; translation mine).

[10]This stance was by no means restricted to the Italian theatrical tradition. For example, Stephen Orgel has argued that Shakespeare's drama creates an argument, not a plot: "This is what critics from Horace to Castelvetro and Sidney mean when they say that mimesis is only the means of drama, not its end. Its end, they assume, is the same as the end of poetry and the other verbal arts—to persuade" (1983, 44). If one keeps such expectations in mind, then the quality of *Aminta*'s characters becomes an advantage, rather than a liability.

[11]Here it is worth mentioning the deeply split relationship between Church authorities and the stage: while using it for educational purposes in their *oratoria* and schools (see chapter one of Vignati 1991), they condemned actors and actresses for luring their spectators to the devil by way of their Proteus-like ability to change their appearance. Even secular authorities were at times rather unkind vis-à-vis street performers such as those of the *commedia dell'arte* troupes: see Taviani and Schino 1982, particularly 379–86, where they explain in detail the confrontation that took place in Milan in 1581 between

The epideictic origin and goal of pastorals such as *Aminta* emerge even more powerfully if we concentrate on the privileged space of court performances. Often Tasso's pastoral was enriched on stage by the addition of other, "minor" events, called *intermezzi*, that are of paramount importance to theatre historians trying to understand how sense was created at the time. *Intermezzi* were usually written specifically for a single performance; normally, they contained direct references to the occasion being celebrated at court. These text-based events, much like masques at the Elizabethan and Jacobean British court, could not be repeated because references to the occasion were too rife to adapt them to other settings. *Intermezzi* were almost certainly nonreferential; performers spent much time pointing out the identity and the circumstances of their characters. At times, although not as frequently as in Britain, *intermezzi* were performed by members of the ruler's household or court. Mostly, though, they were set to music (for the 1628 Parma performance of *Aminta* no less a composer than Claudio Monteverdi worked on the score for the *intermezzi*, which unfortunately is lost), so they required the singing abilities of professionals.

Intermezzi were often more successful than the main pastoral because the latter held no surprise as far as the plot was concerned,[12] and it was only indirectly linked to the occasion being celebrated. The *intermezzi* became more interesting than the main text itself partly because they effectively bridged the events on the stage and those being celebrated in "real" life.[13] Traditionally, though, Tasso's *intermezzi* have been omitted from modern *Aminta* printings due to a classicizing tendency and a deep misunderstanding of the nature of staged entertainment. The edi-

---

the local bishop, St. Carlo Borromeo, and the Gelosi company. It is less probable that courtly performances were employed to avoid the strict censorship imposed on the printing press; indeed, the very space in which they took place was rigorously regulated.

[12]An extant letter regarding the 1628 performance of *Aminta* is quite explicit on this issue: "the play was recognized as *Aminta* and for this reason the audience did not listen to it attentively" (Minucci 1885, 562; translation mine); "by the fifth act the actors realized that the audience was not following them and so delivered it in great haste" (Minucci 1885, 564; translation mine).

[13]While de' Sommi, probably in the 1560s, praises the innovation of the *intermezzi* as "necessary" to a play to "give some distraction to the minds of the audience members" and to help the playwright bestow the sense of time passing on the various events of the acts of the main play (1968, 56; translation mine); in 1598 Ingegneri condemns them for tragedies (as they disrupt the dramatic tension of the main text) and barely accepts them for comedies and pastorals: "[T]hey are not suitable to comedies and pastorals, but they adorn them greatly; whether similar or dissimilar from the main plot, they always enrich the show and entertain the audience" (1974, 282; translation mine).

tor of the most recent critical edition of *Aminta,* Bartolo Tommaso Sozzi, included the choruses but excluded the *intermezzi* and the epilogue from the text of the play. He based his choice on a generalized appreciation for simplicity and linearity, which he projects on Tasso himself. In Sozzi's opinion the *intermezzi* are but lyrical passages adapted by Tasso to the text of the play "for a merely practical and extrinsic goal, and in a temporary manner" (1949, 427; translation mine). Moreover, in his opinion "it is impossible to verify for which performance Tasso wrote them" (1949, 428 n. 1; translation mine).

Generally, *intermezzi* have been badly miscast and misunderstood because the events on stage have been poorly reconstructed. For example, Marzia Pieri asserts that the *intermezzi* of the spectacles taking place in Florence in 1586 and 1589, under Bernardo Buontalenti's direction, employed "stage machinery that ambitiously represents a totalizing reality rich in subtle, fascinating philosophical suggestions. The stage becomes a magic box which dazzles and changes all the time, involving all five senses (even flavors and smells are included). This mechanism is still compact but it is fatally destined to dissolve in a mechanical, gratuitous multiplicity of forms. Such will be the baroque apparatus of melodrama, where scene changes in full view will be simply a part of the repertory and utterly self-serving" (1989, 97; translation mine).

Pieri's assertion reflects a bias against the baroque that has pervaded the Italian critical tradition after Benedetto Croce's idealistic influence. Despite this bias, however, Pieri cannot fail to recognize at least in the pre-baroque period of the 1580s the fascination that stage machinery, ever-changing scenography, and what we would call "special effects" produced on the audience. The goal is obvious: enthralling and fascinating the audience, so that it would be captivated by the staging. This is a first important sense in which Pieri's assessment of scene changes as self-serving is misguided. Moreover, if the audience is enthralled and held captive by the performance, then the message will be effectively delivered and the epideictic task accomplished. At that moment, the dazzling, bewildering staging of the *intermezzi* will not simply satisfy the audience's desire for novelty; it will also convey the deeper meaning of the event. It is worth recalling that, while an "official" plot might have been suggested to the author(s) of the *intermezzi,* the ruler was also a part of the audience. As such, he would have been subject to the same effects as everyone else there. Therefore, one cannot merely talk of "imposition" of a privileged meaning on the audience or even less of "manipulation."

Another such inadequate judgment is expressed by Elena Povoledo in her important 1969 essay on Italian scenography. In her opinion, *in-*

termezzi play a multiple role: they "bind the continuity of the show, by then called 'unity of action' by the renewed Aristotelian polemic; justify the passing of time; distract the audience from the actions of the servants that were on stage [in between acts], while also diverting its attention from the long, compulsory stay in the theatre" (449; translation mine). First of all, the *intermezzi* do not aim at binding together the various parts of the entertainment. Indeed, the very fact that they do not share a plot but are freestanding emphasizes their discontinuity. In this respect, *intermezzi* elicited the delighted response of an audience that wanted to be amazed by something new all the time. Moreover, since the stage is occupied by the performers of the *intermezzi,* no stagehand can work to remove the props needed in one scene and to replace them with those required for a subsequent one. Last, late Renaissance audiences did not seem to be bothered by a lengthy show; it was quite ordinary for an evening of theatrical entertainment to last six or seven hours. Thus, they did not need to find solace from it.[14]

The *intermezzi* were key elements in making the pastoral relevant to its audience after the first few performances. If the audience, as I mentioned, needed to be perennially amazed by novel events or technical artifices, it is because its "willing suspension of disbelief" did not include its personal knowledge vis-à-vis the events on stage. This is indeed one of the aspects that differs the most from twentieth-century conventions, where "members of the audience in their capacity as onlookers, as official eavesdroppers, are accorded by the playwright a specific information state relative to the inner events of the drama, and this state necessarily is different from the playwright's and in all likelihood different from that of various characters in the play. . . . Being part of the audience in a theatre obliges us to act as if our own knowledge, as well as that of some of the characters, is partial" (Goffman 1974, 135).

For a pastoral audience to fully enjoy the show, they needed to experience a sense of utter novelty vis-à-vis what was taking place on stage. De' Sommi recognized this need: "If possible, I would stage a new play,

---

[14]Extant documents concerning the 1628 *Aminta* staging at Parma indicate that the performance lasted approximately eight hours. Having said this, it is important to underline that the complaints about the evening did not involve its length, the quality of the acting, or the comfort of the seating; rather, they revolved around the fact that audience members had become chilled to the bones sitting in a temporary structure with only a partial roof on a cold December night in Northern Italy (see for example Minucci 1885, 563–64).

or at least one that is not well known. I would avoid plays that have been printed as much as possible, no matter how beautiful, because people like what is new better; and also because it is commonly held that audiences do not favor those plays that are already known, for a number of reasons" ([1560?] 1968, 38; translation mine). Chief among these reasons is the excessive effort required by the performers to convince the audience of the truth of the events. Such effort emerged as strained. The notion of pretending to have forgotten characters and events was completely foreign to the people attending these theatrical spectacles, so *intermezzi* added novelty to an already-seen play. Additionally, *intermezzi* played the crucial role of connecting the events on the stage to what was being celebrated and to the everyday reality of the courtiers. In other words, *intermezzi* constituted an important signal pointing to the concrete relevance of the pastoral. Because they are strongly linked to the occasion celebrated with each staging at court, they are subtracted from the frame of make-believe that characterizes twentieth-century stagings. Instead, they belong to the frame of the ritual: "Like scripted productions, a whole mesh of acts are plotted in advance, rehearsal of what is to unfold can occur, and an easy distinction can be drawn between rehearsal and 'real' performance. But whereas in stage plays this preformulation allows for a broad simulation of ordinary life, in ceremonials it functions to constrict, allowing one deed, one doing, to be stripped from the usual texture of events and choreographed to fill out a whole occasion. In brief, a play keys life, a ceremony an event" (Goffman 1974, 58).

Not only do the *intermezzi* contribute to emphasizing the occasion at hand so as to enhance its significance, they also increase the relevance of the pastoral for its audience, thus contributing to carrying out the play's epideictic function. Far from undermining the significance of *Aminta*, its *intermezzi* contributed to the flexibility that assured its continuous popularity on courtly stages for a remarkably long time; indeed, they contributed decisively to the irony of *Aminta* being performed too often for its own good, as the evidence from the 1628 Parma celebration declares.

By connecting staged performances with their occasion, the *intermezzi* help twentieth-century scholars understand the relevance that such events had for their contemporaries. At the same time, they help us to understand how concrete their epideictic force was for their audiences, who approached them as relevant to everyday existence and not as mere *divertissements*. Unless we place suitable importance on a rhetorical approach to Renaissance and early baroque pastoral productions, we will be utterly unable to understand their importance, assess their impact, or explore the process through which they created meaning for their intended audience.

Works Cited

Aristotle. 1960. *The Rhetoric*. Englewood Cliffs: Prentice-Hall.

Cruciani, Fabrizio. 1985. "Percorsi critici verso la prima rappresentazione dell'*Aminta*." In *Torquato Tasso tra letteratura musica teatro e arti figurative*, ed. Andrea Buzzoni, 179–92. Milan: Nuova Alfa.

Cruciani, Fabrizio, and Daniele Seragnoli, eds. 1987. *Il teatro italiano nel Rinascimento*. Bologna: Il mulino.

Curtius, Ernst Robert. [1953] 1983. *European Literature and the Latin Middle Ages*. Princeton: Princeton University Press.

Della Terza, Dante. 1980. "La corte e il teatro: il mondo del Tasso." In *Il teatro italiano del Rinascimento*, ed. Maristella de Panizza Lorch, 51–63. Milan: Edizioni di Comunità.

de' Sommi, Leone. [1560?] 1968. *Quattro dialoghi in materia di rappresentazioni sceniche*, ed. Ferruccio Marotti. Milan: Il polifilo.

Donadoni, Eugenio. 1952. *Torquato Tasso. Saggio critico*. Florence: La Nuova Italia.

Fubini, Mario. 1971. *Studi sulla letteratura del Rinascimento*. Florence: La Nuova Italia.

Godard, Alain. 1977. "La Première représentation de l'*Aminta:* la cour de Ferrare et son double." In *Ville et campagne dans la littérature italienne de la Renaissance. II: Le Courtisan travesti*, ed. André Rochon, 187–301. Paris: Université de la Sorbonne Nouvelle.

Goffman, Erving. [1974] 1986. *Frame Analysis. An Essay on the Organization of Experience*. Boston: Northeastern University Press.

Habermas, Jürgen. [1962] 1989. *The Structural Transformation of the Public Sphere. An Inquiry into a Category of Bourgeois Society*. Cambridge: MIT Press.

Ingegneri, Angelo. [1598] 1974. *Della poesia rappresentativa e del modo di rappresentare le favole sceniche*. In *Lo spettacolo dall'Umanesimo al Manierismo*, ed. Ferruccio Marotti, 271–308. Milan: Feltrinelli.

Minucci del Rosso, P. 1885. "Le nozze di Margherita de' Medici con Odoardo Farnese duca di Parma e Piacenza. Parte II." *Rassegna nazionale* 7, no. 22:550–70.

Orgel, Stephen. 1983. "Shakespeare Imagines a Theater." In *Shakespeare: Man of the Theater*, ed. Kenneth Muir, 34–46. Newark: University of Delaware Press.

Pieri, Marzia. 1989. *La nascita del teatro moderno in Italia tra XV e XVI secolo*. Turin: Bollati Boringhieri.

Povoledo, Elena. 1969. "Origini e aspetti della scenografia in Italia dalla fine del Quattrocento agli intermezzi fiorentini del 1589." In *Li due Orfei. Da Poliziano a Monteverdi*, ed. Nino Pirrotta, 371–509. Turin: ERI.

Prodi, Paolo. 1965. "Ricerche sulla teorica delle arti figurative nella Riforma cattolica." *Archivio italiano per la storia della pietà* 4:121–212.

Solerti, Angelo. 1895. *Vita di Torquato Tasso.* Turin: Loescher.

Sozzi, Bartolo Tommaso. 1949. "Nota sui cori e sugl'intermedi dell'*Aminta.*" *Giornale storico della letteratura italiana* 126:426–31.

Taviani, Ferdinando, and Mirella Schino. 1982. *Il segreto della commedia dell'arte.* Florence: La casa Usher.

Vickers, Brian. 1983. "Epideictic and Rhetoric in the Renaissance." *New Literary History* 14:497–537.

Vignati, Laura. 1991. *Storia delle filodrammatiche negli oratori milanesi dalle origini ai nostri giorni.* Milan: FOM.

Whigham, Frank. 1983. "Interpretation at Court: Courtesy and the Performer-Audience Dialectic." *New Literary History* 14:623–39.

Shakespeare's Rhetoric versus

the Ideology of

Ian McKellen's *Richard III*

George L. Geckle

N *Richard III,* Shakespeare's rhetoric—his conscious and deliberate use of the arts of language for persuasion—is clearly intended to characterize the protagonist of the play as an inherently evil
man whose own use of rhetoric enables him to rise to the position of
king of England. Shakespeare's agenda, if we may use that currently
fashionable critical term, is to represent Richard, Duke of Gloucester,
as a villain and a tyrant and to establish Henry, Earl of Richmond, the
future Henry VII and grandfather of Queen Elizabeth I, as a hero and
savior of the realm. Whereas for Shakespeare the historical process
known to us as the Wars of the Roses ends in 1485 with the glorious
victory of Henry over Richard at the battle of Bosworth Field, the
1990s version of the play, first conceived by Richard Eyre (Director of
London's Royal National Theatre), ends with the implication that the
process did not end in 1485 or even in the 1930s. Both McKellen's
stage version, directed by Eyre, and his film version, directed by Richard
Loncraine, attempt to promote an ideology—that is, a construction of
reality for social and political purposes (see Montrose 1992, 396)—that
offers a radical critique of the British upper classes. This 1990s *Richard
III* is both an interpretation of Shakespeare's play and a rhetorical attempt to undermine royalist ideology.

Shakespeare clearly indicates as early as *3 Henry VI* (ca. 1589–92)
what the audience is to think of Richard, Duke of Gloucester. The
playwright gives Richard a soliloquy at the end of act 3, scene 2 in
which the would-be king expresses his desire to attain the English
crown and notes the obstacles in his way, including King Henry VI
and his son, Edward, as well as Richard's own brothers, Edward and

Clarence, and, as Richard puts it, "all the unlooked-for issue of their bodies" (3.2.131). He himself points out that his appearance prevents him from being a ladies' man, as is his brother Edward. In an extraordinary passage Richard describes the reason for his deformity and what he looks like:

> Why, love forswore me in my mother's womb;
> And, for I should not deal in her soft laws,
> She did corrupt frail nature with some bribe,
> To shrink mine arm up like a withered shrub;
> To make an envious mountain on my back,
> Where sits deformity to mock my body;
> To shape my legs of an unequal size;
> To disproportion me in every part,
> Like to a chaos, or an unlicked bear whelp
> That carries no impression like the dam.
> And am I then a man to be beloved?
> O monstrous fault, to harbor such a thought!
> (3.2.153–64)

There is no self-pity here, just a blunt, matter-of-fact awareness of his own nature, delivered in richly figurative language and concluding with one of Richard's typical rhetorical questions and answers.

In case the audience misses the point, Richard goes on to say that he does not yet know how to get the crown but is capable of both violence—"[I] Torment myself to catch the English crown; / And from that torment I will free myself / Or hew my way out with a bloody axe" (3.2.179–81)—and guile—"Why, I can smile, and murder whiles I smile" (182) and even "set the murderous Machiavel to school" (193). No Elizabethan audience could fail to catch the anachronistic but ominous allusion to the greatest contemporary demon of them all, the Italian Niccolò Machiavelli, author of *The Prince* (1532) and the founder of what we now call modern political science. And, of course, in act 5, scene 5 of *3 Henry VI*, Richard proves what he is capable of when he participates with his brothers, Edward and Clarence, in stabbing King Henry's young son Edward to death at the Battle of Tewkesbury and then in 5.6 goes by himself to the Tower of London and dispatches the King.

Richard's last speech in scene 6 is a soliloquy over the dead body of King Henry in which he again defines himself in no uncertain terms as someone who possesses "neither pity, love, nor fear" (5.6.68), someone who was born "with my legs forward" (71), and, moreover, "born with teeth" (75): "Then, since the heavens have shaped my body so, / Let hell make crook'd my mind to answer it" (78–79). These soliloquies are designed by Shakespeare to reflect the Neoplatonic notion that the exterior is a reflection of the interior, that the body mirrors the soul, a concept that Shakespeare evokes again in *Measure for Measure* (1604) when the Duke compliments Isabella: "The hand that hath made you fair hath made you good" and "grace, being the soul of your complexion, shall keep the body of it ever fair" (3.1.182–83, 184–85).

That the audience is to remain certain about Richard's character and intentions is, I take it, the reason that Shakespeare opens *Richard III* (ca. 1592–94) with Richard's famous soliloquy beginning, "Now is the winter of our discontent / Made glorious summer by this sun of York" (1.1.1–2). It is a rhetorically powerful speech full of tropes—such as the metaphorical uses of "winter" and "summer"—and figures or schemes—such as the pun, technically termed syllepsis, on "sun [that is, sun/son] of York"—in which Richard again describes his physical deformity—"not shaped for sportive tricks" (1.1.14), "rudely stamped" (16), "curtailed of . . . fair proportion" (18), "Cheated of feature by dissembling Nature / Deformed, unfinished" (19–20)—and plans: "I am determinèd to prove a villain / And hate the idle pleasures of these days. / Plots have I laid, inductions dangerous . . . " (30–32). Richard's rhetorical skills and deviousness, not his military ability, enable him to attain the crown. This point is underscored in the second scene with Richard's utterly improbable but successful wooing of Lady Anne, widow of Edward, Prince of Wales, whom Richard helped to kill at Tewkesbury. Even Richard is astounded at this victory, gained during the funeral procession and over the hearse of the very King Henry that he himself killed in the Tower of London: "Was ever woman in this humor [i.e., choleric] wooed? / Was ever woman in this humor won?" (1.2.230–31). The two lines of blank verse, displaying anaphora and parison (see Vickers 1971, 87), as well as alliteration and irony in the form of two rhetorical questions, exemplify Richard's rhetorical brilliance and clever wit.

Part of Richard's appeal to both actors and, at least initially, to audiences is his letting us in on the delight he takes in his cleverness and duplicity, as at the end of the family gathering in act 1, scene 3 (during the course of which he attacks Queen Elizabeth for both her low birth and the imprisonment of Clarence and is in turn attacked by both Elizabeth and Queen Margaret, the widow of Henry VI):

> I do the wrong, and first begin to brawl.
> The secret mischiefs that I set abroach
> I lay unto the grievous charge of others.

Clarence, who I indeed have cast in darkness,
I do beweep to many simple gulls—
Namely to Derby, Hastings, Buckingham—
And tell them 'tis the Queen and her allies
That stir the King against the Duke my brother.
Now they believe it, and withal whet me
To be revenged on Rivers, Dorset, Grey,
But then I sigh and, with a piece of Scripture,
Tell them that God bids us do good for evil.
And thus I clothe my naked villainy
With odd old ends stol'n forth of Holy Writ,
And seem a saint when most I play the devil.
                                                                    (1.3.324–38)

Richard's reference to himself as an actor playing the devil is repeated later in an aside during an exchange with young Prince Edward:

RICHARD [*aside*]: So wise, so young, they say, do never live long.

PRINCE EDWARD: What say you, uncle?

RICHARD: I say, without characters fame lives long.
[*aside*] Thus, like the formal Vice, Iniquity,
I moralize two meanings in one word.
                                                                    (3.1.79–83)

The play on the meaning of "without characters" (i.e., even without written records and even without moral character) is another example of the rhetorical figure syllepsis, but even more important than the rhetorical cleverness is Richard's self-identification with the Vice figure of medieval drama.

Richard's ability to "seem a saint when most I play the devil" is nowhere more evident than in several crucial scenes in act 3, such as scene 4, where he first stage-manages with the help of Buckingham the demise of Hastings by accusing Hastings of protecting his mistress Jane Shore, who supposedly with Queen Elizabeth had used witchcraft to wither Richard's left arm. In the climactic scene 7, Buckingham in turn stage-manages the acclamation of the mayor and citizens of London—"And look you get a prayer book in your hand, / And stand between two churchmen" (3.7.47–48), he instructs Richard—so that Richard is proclaimed King.

It is, of course, soon after the coronation in scene 2 of act 4 that things begin to go wrong for Richard, as even Buckingham demurs when Richard tells him that he wishes the young princes killed. In Shakespeare's text not even James Tyrrel—who gets a greatly expanded role as chief assassin in McKellen's film version—is able to execute the deed, and he bribes two others, Dighton and Forrest, "To do," as Tyrrel says, "this piece of ruthless butchery" (4.3.5). Tyrrel's subsequent description of the murders is clearly designed by Shakespeare to evoke such pathos that no member of the audience can possibly feel any rapport with Richard from then on. When Richard's own mother curses him in scene 4—"Thou cam'st on earth to make the earth my hell. / A grievous burden was thy birth to me; / Tetchy and wayward was thy infancy; / Thy schooldays frightful, desperate, wild, and furious" (4.4.167–70)—we are not meant to pity him as a victim of child abuse, a concept that both Eyre and McKellen invoke in their interpretation of his character, as I document below. Nor when Richard wakes screaming in 5.3 from the nightmarish vision of the eight sets of ghosts who deliver the refrain "Despair and die!" are we to feel sorry for him. Nor in act 5 when he exits screaming "A horse! A horse! My kingdom for a horse!" (5.4.13) are we to feel sorry for him. What we are supposed to feel, I would argue, is relief that, as the victorious Richmond puts it, "the bloody dog is dead" (5.5.2), and joy that Richmond and Elizabeth of York will upon their imminent marriage "unite the white rose [of York] and the red [of Lancaster]" (19). This event will usher in a future of "smooth-faced peace, / With smiling plenty, and fair prosperous days!" (33–34), right down to the early 1590s when Queen Elizabeth, granddaughter of Richmond, who became King Henry VII, was herself sitting on the English throne and no doubt at some point also attending a performance of this very play.

And now for the rest of the story . . .

The Royal National Theatre's *Richard III*, starring Ian McKellen, opened at the Lyttelton Theatre on 25 July 1990 and then went on world tour from September 1990 through March 1991. It reopened in May 1992 at the Lyttelton and then went on U.S. tour from June to September, the first major RNT production to tour the U.S. All told, there were over three hundred performances of this highly successful *Richard III*.

One of its major differences from recent twentieth-century productions of the play is that it is set in the 1930s. In an interview in the *New York Times,* Richard Eyre explained the ideological basis of his interpretive approach. First of all it was political; second, it was based on modern sociological and psychological assumptions; and third, it was about issues of class. In terms of politics, its avid reception in Bucharest "was particularly important to Mr. Eyre, because he often visited the city in the Ceaucescu [*sic*] period and had Romania as much in mind as England when he and Mr. McKellen began to discuss the production. 'To me it isn't a play about medieval tyranny and the Yorkists and Lancastrians,' he said. 'To me, it's indelibly a model of tyranny in our own times, a prototype for the one political form that's been perfected in the 20th century' " (Nightingale 5).

In a special program designed for the U.S. tour, Eyre was interviewed (by Dominique Goy-Blanquet) for an extensive five-page essay titled "Directing *Richard III*." He elaborated on the point that the play is "a model of tyranny in our own times": "The rise of a dictator and the political thuggery that goes with it are the main topics of the play. We did not have to look far for analogies: the twentieth century has sophisticated tyranny beyond the dreams of the previous two millennia and the examples close to us were embarrassingly rich. I had a first-hand, if vicarious, knowledge of tyranny through strong personal ties of friendship in Romania, where I had been many times before the revolution, but we never sought to establish literal equivalents between mediaeval and modern tyrants" (1992, n.p.).

Although there were no "literal equivalents" between Richard III and, say, Nicolae Ceausescu, the production had, it seems, particular relevance for the Romanians, who received it with enthusiasm when the company played at their National Theatre 15–18 February 1991. Ian McKellen told J. Wynn Rousuck of the *Baltimore Sun* (21 June 1992) that "When we did the play in Romania recently, the audience thought it was all about Ceausescu. . . . When we did it in Hamburg, they thought it was the Third Reich, and people say, have I based my performance on Saddam Hussein? I haven't, but if that's what it looks like, that's fine. It proves we have gotten to the heart of a dictator" (Rousuck 1). Brian Cox, who played the Duke of Buckingham in London and the world tour performances, makes a similar observation in his book *The Lear Diaries:* "In Prague and even more so in Bucharest I see where Richard Eyre's inspiration lies for his production of *Richard III*. Whatever reservations I have about the production it is quite clear the effect the performance has on audiences in the Eastern bloc and it validates the whole conception" (Cox 1992, 202).

But "the whole conception" also created doubts and problems for some reviewers in London and the U.S., although others thought it was highly successful, and just about everybody who saw the play remarked on the specific analogies between Eyre's production and the rise of fascism in the 1930s. Eyre himself admitted these connections in the interview "Directing *Richard III*": "We did draw some parallels with the rise of Hitler, or the influence of Oswald Mosley in 1930s England, but these specific co-ordinates are tagged on to timeless references. To me, the play is set in a mythological landscape, even if it draws on a historically precise period. Audiences who restrict this landscape to Nazi imagery are too literal-minded. There is *no* Nazi imagery" (1992, n.p.). Perhaps so, but audiences and reviewers were certainly led by both the original RNT London program and the U.S. program to believe that the production had something specifically to do with the Nazis as well as Mosley. Both programs contained quotations from Hermann Goering and Adolf Hitler, as well as Mosley (and Joseph Stalin). Moreover, both programs featured reproductions of Hubert Lanzinger's "The Standard-bearer," a portrait of Hitler in which the Führer is represented in medieval-like armor on horseback holding a flag with a swastika. This painting, we are told, "was personally selected by Hitler as the official painting of the Führer for the Great German Art Exhibition, 1938, in the House of German Art." The London production's depiction of Richard accepting the crown at the end of 3.7 included clear parallels to Hitler's mass rallies, complete with armbands, Sieg Heil-type chants, microphones, and spotlights. Perhaps most symbolic, however, was the massive backdrop cloth that unfurled at Richard's coronation (4.2), revealing a nude (and not deformed but, in fact, athletic, Aryan-looking) McKellen on a white horse, the actor, with right arm raised, holding a standard with an emblem of St. George.

In a program for the 1995 film version of the production, the connection with Hitler is made even clearer: "The barren, concrete lower levels [of Earls Court Exhibition Center] provided the behind-the-scenes area of the arena where Richard held a Nuremberg style rally. . . . Richard's military headquarters were filmed at Steam Town, a train museum at Carnforth in Lancashire. In a touch of irony, the filmmakers utilized a German engine which was originally designed to pull Hitler's train" (United Artists Pictures Program 1995, 11).

Finally, in the London program Barbara Everett of Oxford University equates insatiable hunger for power with the inevitability of self-destruction: "This climb to the throne is the subject of *Richard III*. And the dramatist's theme, the seizing of power, is so lucidly embodied as to make his play an archetype, a pattern by which to recognise all later power-politics. It's hardly surprising that Brecht's play about how to become a Hitler, *The Resistible Rise of Arturo Ui*, takes off from *Richard III*. . . . In the Book of Revelation, Death enters on a pale horse. With something of the same nightmarish intensity Richard moves into battle at Bosworth on his charger, 'White Surrey', and dies shouting 'My kingdom for a horse'. In the dream-horse that doesn't come at all ['Give me another horse!' 5.3.177] there is some odd hint of the uncontrollable energies of the human animal that lives simply for power" (1990, n.p.). In the RNT stage version, Richard, Richmond, and the others all wore medieval armor and fought with swords at Bosworth Field, but in the film version, with its consistent attempt at verisimilitude, the anachronism of the thirties setting is made ludicrously evident when Richard shouts his most famous line—"A horse! A horse! My kingdom for a horse!"—while in a jeep stuck in the dirt.

Some London reviewers, such as the *Guardian*'s Michael Billington and the *Independent*'s Paul Taylor, bought Everett's view that the play (and production) is about the instinct for power; others, such as the *Times*'s Robert Hewison, the *Financial Times*'s Martin Hoyle, and the *Daily Telegraph*'s Charles Osborne read the programmatic signposts differently and thought that the parallels with 1930s Europe were too insistently drawn. Osborne put it trenchantly: " . . . this Richard [in 3.7] becomes Adolph Hitler in black shirt and jackboots, or possibly Doctor Strangelove, his arm taking unilateral action in a Nazi salute. Earlier, he seemed briefly to have been Enoch Powell, and in his coronation there is more than a hint of Edward VIII. Joyce Redman's Duchess of York, meanwhile, has progressed sartorially from the present Queen Mother to George V's Queen Mary. . . . George V is present, too, in the person of Brian Cox's Buckingham (or Bucking-*Ham,* as this Richard unkindly calls him)" (16). In the film version, with the costumes, according to the program, "very specific to 1936" (United Artists Pictures Program 1995, 9), the differences between the 1480s and 1930s are totally obscured, and executive producer Ellen Dinerman Little indicates that the American actress Annette Bening, who plays Edward's Queen Elizabeth, is modeled on "Wallis Warfield Simpson, for whom Edward VIII abdicated the throne in the 1930s" (7). Perhaps the most telling criticism of the conception came from Lloyd Rose (who saw the stage production approximately two years later at the John F. Kennedy Center for the Performing Arts) in the *Washington Post* of 25 June 1992 when he argued that Eyre "doesn't draw his images from the text, he slathers them on top of it. All the work is being done by the set, lighting and sound designers. If you give what's going on a moment's thought, you wonder how on Earth the threat of fascism applies to internecine wars among a hereditary monarchy, a system that pretty much guaranteed a succession of rulers whom today we'd judge as tyrants" (2). Rose's criticism raises serious questions about Eyre's politically based ideological interpretive strategy.

Eyre's second major conception, sociologically and psychologically based, came from readings of the opening speech of the play—"Now is the winter of our discontent"—which, says Benedict Nightingale, "convinced Mr. Eyre that it was less a hunchback's bitter complaint against nature than an army officer's lament over the coming of peace. Moreover, the research he had done for 'Tumbledown,' a television film he had made about the war in the Falkland Islands and its aftermath, had shown him that crippled soldiers desperately conceal rather than parade their disabilities. Therefore, Ian McKellen would not play Richard as a deformed monster, as most actors do. 'He's semi-paralyzed; he only uses one arm, but he's doing his best to insure we don't notice it' " (5). In his interview/essay "Directing *Richard III*," Eyre elaborated on Richard's physical handicaps: "In our production, Ian McKellen plays Richard with a slightly twisted spine, he has chronic alopecia [i.e., loss of hair], and he is paralysed down one side of his body. These three handicaps taken together are quite sufficient to account for all the abuse he attracts. Experience shows that even slight deformities are enough to inspire revulsion. Modern reactions to disability have not changed so very much in this respect."

"Experience" and "modern reactions," however, are not, I would argue, sufficient reason to ignore the very specific references in both *3 Henry VI* and *Richard III* to the severe deformities of Richard. McKellen may have had a particular desire to conceal the deformities as much as possible in order to make his Richard compellingly different from previous famous characterizations by Laurence Olivier and Antony Sher, even though he has said that this is not the case: "It was not a conscious choice to do it differently from those distinguished predecessors. . . . Richard cannot be as deformed as his enemies say he is, because he was first and foremost a soldier and would have had to be involved in combat. I actually present him with a considerable handicap—he has a distorted spine, he is ugly from the side where his face is blasted and his hair doesn't grow properly—but you don't see much of it because he spends his time covering it up, as many people who have a deformity do" (Raymond 1992, 13). In the film version McKellen reduces the physical defects even more, so that Richard has a normal head of hair.

Eyre, however, gives the game away when he tells us (in "Directing *Richard III*"): "Laurence Olivier's interpretation has become central to the mythology of the play, but the deformity he depicts is unbelievable when you think that Richard has fought well in so many battles" (1992, n.p.). Yet Shakespeare, at least in *Richard III*, indicates that Richard fights on horseback—"Saddle white Surrey for the field tomorrow" (5.3.64)—until he loses his horse and is slain while on foot. McKellen clearly wanted to do a different, nontraditional Richard, as he told Gerard Raymond: "He is a man who has had to take control of himself against the most enormous physical odds. And that willpower allows him to fight his way to the top, just as it allowed him to fight successfully on the battlefield" (1992, 13). Of course, the ghosts of Richard's victims in 5.3 give a rather different slant to what McKellen's sentimental "fight his way to the top" really means. Nonetheless, the way McKellen characterized Richard impressed many reviewers (as it did me) because of his almost hypnotic self-control and seemingly magical feats of dexterity with his good right arm and hand, including the putting on of gloves and the lighting of cigarettes (one of Richard's major props in this production).

Eyre's and McKellen's more compelling reason for deemphasizng Richard's disabilities may well be that they seem to have approached the play from a modern psychoanalytic perspective. Eyre hints at this in "Directing *Richard III*" when he tells us that Richard "had to fight against so many odds. He is the youngest son, coming after two very strong, dominant, assertive brothers, and he is crippled." Moreover, Richard's mother, asserts Eyre, "has despised him from birth and says so unequivocally to Clarence's children. Because we were going on a world tour and could not take so many young people along with us, I had to leave these children out, and I ran the two family scenes of the first act [he meant 1.3 and 2.2] into one. So the Duchess comes in earlier, she is present at the dynastic family reunion [in 1.3], and her words of contempt are spoken in Richard's hearing. It is a fair assumption that she has always treated him in this way. Whether we take evil to be an innate spiritual force, or merely a matter of psychological conditioning, there is sufficient evidence for both views in the play" (1992, n.p.).

There is, of course, hardly any notion of "psychologial conditioning" in Shakespeare's text, which, rather, reflects the Neoplatonic concept of the body as a reflection of the soul. McKellen, less equivocal than Eyre, told Jeff Bradley: "It's positively amazing that, so many years before psychoanalysis, he [Shakespeare] understood so well how a boy born with a terrible deformity would become a terrible tyrant. One sees that he's unloved and unlovable." McKellen concluded, therefore, that the Duchess of York was the culprit: "Olivier cut the mother out of his movie. But she parades her hatred for her son and one begins to see that the boy put up with so much as a youngster, it was no wonder he turned out as he did" (Bradley 1992, 7). McKellen added the following variation on this theme in the interview with Gerard Raymond: "His mother hates him simply because he is deformed. There is no man in the world who can recover from that" (1992, 14).

This psychoanalytic interpretation may have come from a study of Antony Sher's approach to Richard, demonstrated in detail by Hugh

M. Richmond in his *Shakespeare in Performance: "King Richard III"* (110–12), although, of course McKellen might argue that it was "not a conscious choice" (Raymond 1992, 13). But then McKellen also tells us in his essay, "Acting *Richard III*," in the special program designed for the U.S. tour that "our production is not an adaptation—nor even an interpretation." Nonetheless, there is surely some sort of interpretation going on when director Richard Eyre tells us in the U.S. program that he "ran the two family scenes of the first act into one" and that the Duchess of York "is present" and "her words of contempt are spoken in Richard's hearing" (1992, n.p.). The words of the Duchess— "He is my son—ay, and therein my shame; / Yet from my dugs he drew not this deceit" (2.2.29–30)—are not spoken in Richard's presence in Shakespeare's text. As scholar Lois Potter has said in a review in *TLS,* "the unloving hero is the product of an unloving mother, herself the product of a social class that refuses to recognize the reality of human emotion" (1990, 825). This statement is true for Eyre's and McKellen's stage version and Loncraine's and McKellen's film version (where the Duchess of York is played by the icily imperious Maggie Smith) but not necessarily for Shakespeare's text, where the chorus of wailing women alone belies the notion that there is some lack of human emotion. This lack of emotion on stage and in film was wonderfully projected by McKellen's use of a Sandhurst accent and rigid military bearing. Irving Wardle noted these characteristics: "McKellen's Richard has a withered arm, but no other conspicuous deformity. It is when he speaks that he becomes a cripple. Like his Iago, this performance is a study in perverted militarism. He has been maimed by upbringing, not nature. Gentrified vowels and barked terminations proclaim a man whose only contact with the human race is through coercion. He delivers soliloquies at attention, and whenever he has a few buttons undone, there is a feverish one-handed return to regimental propriety" (1990, 22).

The issue of class was, in fact, the third key conception behind Eyre's interpretation of the play. As he told Benedict Nightingale, he chose a "distinctively English 30's" setting not "to remind the audience of Edward VIII's less than hostile attitude to Hitler or of the sympathy some aristocrats had for England's leading black shirt, Sir Oswald Mosley" but to highlight the social and cultural issue of class. " 'So much of the play is about class,' said Mr. Eyre. 'The characters are very conscious of whether they are old money or new money. And I said to Ian, suppose we take that to its logical end, and he started to speak in an upper-class accent: "Now is the wintah of our discontent." It was electrifying. Suddenly the play had a real social and political location, and one that fitted with the text, not one we grafted on.' " (Nightingale

1992). As Eyre put it in "Directing *Richard III*," "Queen Elizabeth's family are greedy parvenus," but that is, of course, Richard III's own point against them. Eyre, however, had something larger in mind: "The purpose of the contemporary setting was to show the British aristocracy compounding the rise of such a strong leader. Hastings and Buckingham go along part of the way and stand up too late. Morton, the Bishop of Ely, steers a prudent course which will enable him to remain in power under the Tudors. Stanley also treads a very narrow line. . . . The characters in the play are not in any way ciphers, they have a very fine sense of class and status, they all belong to a manipulative world of high-ranking officials, not a working-class world at all" (Eyre 1992). For Eyre this elitism had contemporary relevance, in spite of the fact that *Richard III* dramatizes the conclusion of the Wars of the Roses, for "the British aristocracy does exercise power in this country, even now, because our class system is kept in place by the presence of the Monarch" (Eyre 1992). It is interesting to learn from Kathleen Tynan in a profile of Eyre that he "comes from an upper-class background, and has rebelled against it; he's a declared republican, and yet leads the Royal National Theater" (Tynan 1992, 17). In short, the Artistic Director of the RNT has a "left-wing allegiance" (21).

Eyre's antiroyalist ideological position was revealed at the end of his production of *Richard III* with the arrival of Richmond against a backdrop of an idealized English countryside dominated by a church. Eyre said in both the U.S. tour program and the profile by Kathleen Tynan that if "asked what I was defending, it would be this idealized picture of England, which to me is more than a metaphor, not an intellectual conceit but literally a heartland" (Tynan 1992, 17). As he has said in "Directing *Richard III*," Edward VIII "was known to harbour sympathy for Mosley's ideas," and the production was "a way of saying that this could have happened, could happen here, even though I would like to believe that the British are inherently immune to fascism" (Eyre 1992). But the ending of his production told us that it "could happen" because Richmond's concluding speech was delivered in front of another emblematic backdrop—this one with Henry VII prominently displayed on it. (The film had nowhere to go with this concept at this point, of course, because of the decision to fight the final battle in modern dress and with WWII military equipment.)

The implication in the stage version was that the process did not end in 1485 or indeed in the 1930s. McKellen says as much in the program for the film version: "There is a wonderful tension in this movie between a history that never happened and what might have happened. Is it credible, could there be such horror going on in such high places? Well, yes:

in this century of tyranny, the 1930s is the most recent period of history when it was possible for an English King to rise to a political dictator" (United Artists Pictures Program 1996, 11). And so we have in Richard Eyre's and Ian McKellen's *Richard III* a decided attempt to offer a radical critique of the British upper classes, an attempt, in fact, to undermine contemporary royalist ideology.

Works Cited

Billington, Michael. 1990. "Enter Richard the Blackshirt." *Guardian,* 27 July, Arts sec., p. 31.

Bradley, Jeff. 1992. "McKellen's Toughest Role in Life." *Denver Post,* Sunday, 7 June, sec. D, pp. 1, 7.

Cox, Brian. 1992. *The Lear Diaries: The Story of the Royal National Theatre's Productions of Shakespeare's* Richard III *and* King Lear. London: Methuen.

Everett, Barbara. 1990. "On a Pale Horse." Royal National Theatre Program [London] for *Richard III.*

Eyre, Richard. 1992. "Directing *Richard III.*" Royal National Theatre Program [U.S.] for *Richard III.*

Hewison, Robert. 1990. "Parallel Portraits Produce a Dark Double Vision." *Sunday Times* (London), 29 July, sec. 5, p. 5.

Hoyle, Martin. 1990. "Richard III." *Financial Times,* 27 July, p. 13.

McKellen, Ian. 1992. "Acting *Richard III.*" Royal National Theatre Program [U.S.] for *Richard III.*

Montrose, Louis. 1992. "New Historicisms." In *Redrawing the Boundaries: The Transformation of English and American Literary Studies,* ed. Stephen Greenblatt and Giles Gunn, 392–418. New York: MLA.

Nightingale, Benedict. 1992. "The Power behind Richard's Throne." *New York Times,* 7 June, sec. 2, p. 5.

Osborne, Charles. 1990. "How to Deform King Richard." *Daily Telegraph,* 27 July, Arts sec., p. 16.

Potter, Lois. 1990. "A Country of the Mind." *TLS,* 3–9 August, 825.

Raymond, Gerard. 1992. "Sir Ian McKellen's *Richard III.*" *Theater Week* 5 (15–21 June): 13–16.

Richmond, Hugh M. 1989. *Shakespeare in Performance:* "King Richard III." Manchester and New York: Manchester University Press.

Rose, Lloyd. 1992. "Tricky 'Richard.' " *Washington Post,* 25 June, sec. C, p. 2.

Rousuck, J. Wynn. 1992. "Ian McKellen Brings Drama of Political Kind to D.C. with Role as Richard III." *Baltimore Sun,* 21 June, sec. J, p. 1.

Shakespeare, William. 1997. *The Complete Works of Shakespeare,* ed. David Bevington. 4th ed., updated. New York: Longman.

Taylor, Paul. 1990. "Playing the Field." *Independent,* 27 July, Arts sec., p. 16.

Tynan, Kathleen. 1992. "Eyre Apparent." *Theater Week* 5 (15–21 June): 17–23.

United Artists Pictures Program for *Richard III*. 1995.

Vickers, Brian. 1971. "Shakespeare's Use of Rhetoric." In *A New Companion to Shakespeare Studies*, ed. Kenneth Muir and S. Schoenbaum. 83–98. Cambridge: Cambridge University Press.

Wardle, Irving. 1990. "Tragic Kings of Misrule." *Independent on Sunday*, 29 July, p. 22.

And Now for Application

Venice Preserv'd and the
Rhetoric of Textual Application

Odai Johnson

It has been observed by others, that this poet [Otway] has founded his
tragedy of *Venice Preserv'd* on so wrong a plot, that the greatest characters in it are those of rebels and traitors.
—Addison, *Spectator,* No. 39, 14 April 1711

I

T WAS AN observation already cliché in Addison's time: there
was no compelling reason why Thomas Otway's *Venice Preserv'd*
should ever have succeeded, founded as it was on "so wrong a plot."
Indeed, given the circumstances of the original production, it had every
reason not to succeed. The play appeared in winter 1681–82, in the
immediate aftermath of the Exclusion Crisis, a Parliamentary campaign to legally exclude the Catholic James, Duke of York, from inher-
iting the throne. The Exclusion Bill of 1681 was initiated by the Whig
party, and after a volatile period of party skirmishes, popish plots, and
insurrection attempts, Charles II dissolved Parliament and effectively
disbanded the Whig party. In the immediate aftermath, court writers
celebrated the defeat of the opposition on stage and in print. *Venice
Preserv'd* belongs to a genre of Tory party propaganda pieces that include John Crowne's *City Politiques* (1683), Thomas D'Urfey's *The Royalist* (1682), and Aphra Behn's *The Roundheads* (1681).

Unlike other Tory plays of the period, however, Otway's insurrection
narrative offered little to recommend it to a king trying to preserve
absolutism against an encroaching parliament and even less to one who
had resolved on ruling without a parliament altogether. Yet Charles II
did indeed endorse the play by attending the poet's night benefit, guar-
anteeing not only the play's success, but its party alignment as well.

Although at one level *Venice Preserv'd* seems to appease royalist sensibilities by presenting a narrative structured around a preserved state and a squashed rebellion, even the most cursory of readings reveals a range of internal ambiguities—so many that, as an allegory of Exclusion politics, the play resists the easy interpretation to which it aspires. Chief among these ambiguities is the preserved state itself, Venice, at the time the most famous republic in Europe. At its titular point of entrance, the play presents an extremely awkward site for royalist propaganda, as the Venice of *Venice Preserv'd* has already abolished its monarchy. Or, at a more immediate level, the play's central character, Jaffier, originally played by the Duke's Company's leading actor, Thomas Betterton, placed the company in the highly schizophrenic position of soliciting sympathy for a romantic hero who was also, unfortunately, a traitor to the state. Romanticizing treason and glorifying conspiracy is further compounded by the nature of the authority that is to be preserved. The Venetian Senate is portrayed as a notoriously corrupt and incompetent body, highlighted in particular by the petty and vindictive Priuli and the perversely lecherous Anthony. (The latter was undoubtedly a broad caricature designed to ridicule Antony Cooper, Earl of Shaftesbury and the head of the Whig party.) A senate represented by two such disreputables raises serious questions about the legitimacy of authority modeled on this state. In the end, one can't help but wonder what exactly is being preserved in *Venice Preserv'd,* and why ever should Charles II have endorsed this play?

It is by no means an original question. Charges of republicanism have haunted the play throughout both its critical and its stage history. Whether Otway's rebellion against the Venetian state represented an endorsement or a parody of the Whig or Tory ascendancy still sustains the debate and still resists easy interpretation. Consequently, more than three hundred years of criticism have produced a considerable range of attempts to disentangle the equivocal party allegiances and allegories. One Otway scholar, Phillip Harth, devoted an entire article to summarizing the most prominent configurations (1988, 345–62).[1] Confront-

---

[1]Other recent treatments include Gerald Parker, "The Image of Rebellion in Thomas Otway's *Venice Preserv'd* and Edward Young's *Busisis,*" *Studies in English Literature, 1500–1900* 21 (1981): 389–407; David Bywater, "Venice, Its Senate, and Its Plot in Otway's *Venice Preserv'd,*" *Modern Philology* 80 (1983): 256–63; Harry M. Solomon, "The Rhetoric of 'Redressing Grievances': Court Propaganda as the Hermeneutical Key to *Venice Preserv'd,*" *ELH* 53 (1986): 289–310; Jessica Munns, " 'Plain as the Light in the Cowcumber': A Note on the Conspiracy in Thomas Otway's *Venice Preserv'd,*" *Modern Philology* 85 (1987): 54–57.

ing such ambiguity led one premiere Otway scholar, Aline Mackenzie
Taylor, to conclude: "The chameleon-like quality of the fable of *Venice
Preserv'd* baffles a reader who seeks to find established in the play itself
the point of view from which the action is to be regarded." (Taylor
1950, 144).[2]

To complicate matters, the stage history of the play seems to bear
out all the instabilities of the text. In politically sensitive times, productions of *Venice Preserv'd* are subjected to the same range of interpretive confusion as the text itself. Let me offer one premiere example.
In the John Kemble production of October 1795, the play's political
speeches elicited a raucous response from dissident members of its audience. Jaffier's seditious passages were successively applauded and berated
by loyalists and detractors of George III, the play's republican tendencies were debated in the papers, disturbances ensued in the house, and
the cry went out that the Drury Lane Theatre was disaffected toward its
government. Kemble toned down the production by replacing Robert
Bensley in the role of the conspirator Pierre with a less-spirited actor,
but the prestidigitation impressed no one. The hostility culminated on
the play's third performance on October 29 with a riot in the theatre. To
quiet the crowd, the orchestra was called to strike up "God Save the
King," an anthem, as James Boaden said, "which implies, in England,
the salvation of everything valuable" (Boaden 1825, I, 519). Yet Kemble's
orchestra was accused of "not playing with sufficient energy," and the
rioting continued. Although the play was drawing large audiences and
earning exceptional receipts, Kemble withdrew it from performance.[3]

It was no fault of the text itself that one very visible parallel was currently playing out just across the channel: the French National Convention was mopping up its own revolution, and the comparison did not
go unnoticed. "Among other strange coincidences," wrote the *Times,*

---

[2]Taylor's is still the most thorough work on the subject. Otway's most recent scholar,
Jessica Munns, cautions: "That *Venice Preserv'd* . . . reflects contemporary politics has
always been acknowledged. What is less clear is how that reflection is to be interpreted"
(*Restoration Politics and Drama: The Plays of Thomas Otway, 1675–1683* [Newark: University of Delaware Press, 1995], 172).

[3]*Morning Chronicle,* 4 November 1795. Press attacks continued into the following
week, citing the same crisis of (mis)interpretation that has remained with the play: "Every
liberal mind must see with disgust the pitiful attempt which is revived by the lowest
retainers of Government to introduce factious politics into our Theatres, and to make the
scene of our rational amusements a forum for the virulence of party. Thus the play of
Venice Preserv'd, the scope of which is to expose the villainy and imbecility of rebellion,
and which a Government willing to repress sedition would desire to bring forward, is to
be thrown aside" (quoted in Taylor, 201).

" . . . let it be ranked that this Play was revived at the very moment when the same parts are acting on the great stage of Paris. Otway has painted the Republican senators of Venice with such a face of absurdity and folly, that, had he written now, one should be tempted to suppose the whole National Convention sat for the picture" (*Times,* 27 October 1795). Yet even here again, in making the analogy, the reviewer inadvertently exposes the cardinal ambiguities of the play by associating the French regicides not with Otway's conspirators, who are assaulting the state of Venice, but with the Senate, the very body that governs Venice. There seems to be an innate and bizarre kink in the narrative loop, a point of slippage in the mobius strip where loyalism is followed until—quite suddenly—it turns traitor; the senators are arraigned, and the conspirators are dismissed. Interpretively speaking, it must have been very difficult for Kemble to anticipate the play's reception.

Nor did it mitigate the ultimate claim that Kemble was using the play to foment rebellion when it was learned that earlier that very day—Thursday, October 29—while King George III was coming from the House of Peers, a bullet shot through his coach, missing the monarch but shattering the glass. A mob followed, wracking the coach and breaking the legs of the king's driver. The *Times* was, again, quick to note the parallel: "The plan of thus insulting his Majesty, and even of taking away his life, follows in close imitation of those horrid events which have disgraced the French Revolution." It is difficult in the press to ascertain exactly which revolution is being addressed. Here the journalist is speaking of the assassination attempt, but he might as well be summarizing *Venice Preserv'd* or, for that matter, Kemble's personal action in producing such a seditious work: "It was there as here, that a few political adventurers summoned the laborious poor from their industrious pursuits to the fields of sedition. . . ." (*Times,* 31 October 1795). The French Revolution, Otway's play, Kemble's production, and the assassination attempt were all bound up in models and actualities of overthrow that are fluidly, coercively read as homogeneous events. In the pages of the *Times,* they freely bleed from subject to subject; indeed, there is such an intertextuality about the events that it becomes sometimes difficult to ascertain which revolution is on the wing. Unfortunately for Kemble, what *Venice Preserv'd* provided was an immediate reprise of a national nightmare of a popular uprising that would culminate in regicide and the installation of a republic, as it had across the channel. That actuality, in the popular imagination, served as a model for assassination. The production thus becomes an aesthetic halfway house between the French Revolution and the would-be English revolution. The model of *Venice Preserv'd,* howsoever unevenly or unfairly it embraced or censured rebellion, nonetheless caught the conscience of the times, and Kemble had little choice but to give o'er the play.

The curious feature, however, of this ongoing interpretive argument is that it is a uniquely post-Restoration problem. From Addison through Kemble to Harth, on page and stage, the sustained and signature commentary on this play—whether the text advocates or condemns rebellion—was remarkably absent when Otway first produced the play in February 1682. There was no question but that it was unmitigated royalism. Charles II attended the poet's benefit, never a blind act (Nicoll 1928, 311). When the city celebrated the homecoming of the king's brother James, Duke of York, with a jubilee feast at the Merchant Taylors Hall, a special production of *Venice Preserv'd* was selected as the culminating course. Again, a month later when the duke's wife, the Duchess Mary, returned to London, Otway's play was chosen as the capstone to the Tory celebration. So here is the question that propelled me through this lengthy prologue: what made the play—the same play—so unabashedly royalist in Otway's original productions and so problematic to post-Restoration readers and audiences?

II: "A silly, useless formality"

One rhetorical device that Restoration playwrights frequently exploited was disappearing by the end of the eighteenth century when Kemble mounted his ill-fated production: the practice of writing prologues and epilogues to frame a production within a unique constellation of performative conditions. As early as 1730 Alexander Pope was complaining, "I have often wished to live to see the day when Prologues and Epilogues should be no more. I wish a Great Genius would break thro' the silly, useless formality" (quoted in Sherburn 1956, IV, 127). Fielding found them so interchangeable he wrote a generalized satire of them all. By midcentury Garrick had revitalized the form, but by Kemble's tenure the practice had again fallen into disuse. Prologues and epilogues were increasingly reserved only for premieres and problem plays, like *Vortigern,* whose writer boasted the play as Shakespeare's and penned a special epilogue to defend the claim. Increasingly, prologues and epilogues were replaced with the playing of "God Save the King." This generic closing piece was the logical culmination of a tired tradition that had played out its usefulness.

But during the Restoration, prologues and epilogues were far from "a silly, useless formality." Bracketing the performance itself, the prologue and epilogue of a Restoration play occupied a unique representational space in the production of the text. Like the Aristophanic parabasis, they offered a direct link from author through actor to audience. Many of Otway's contemporaries exploited the opportunity to exercise an interpretive privilege over the text. For example, Aphra Behn's prologue to *Romulus and Hersillia* (1682) announced the play as locally apolitical ("writ before the times of Whig and Tory"), yet her epilogue posthumously encouraged partisan interpretation, suggesting—facetiously—her Whiggish critics may find in the play's heroine "the first and noblest Whig of Rome" (Wiley 1940, 134). And the first line of Dryden's prologue to *The Duke of Guise* openly declared, "Our play's a Parallel." It then proceeded to map out the correspondences in advance. In the case of a potentially problematic text like *Venice Preserv'd*, a carefully constructed epilogue could not only prevent misinterpretation but could ensure a customized reception.

And so it is not surprising that for each of the three original productions of *Venice Preserv'd*, Otway appended to the performances skillfully fashioned epilogues designed to circumvent any potential misreading by offering an immediate interpretive "key" to the play.[4] Indeed the first epilogue's first line openly, pointedly, announced Otway's hermeneutic objective: "The Text is done, and now for Application." This is a crucial concession for a potentially subversive narrative and a deft move on the playwright's part to suspend closure on the performance until he, the author, could personally "apply" the text. What followed was Otway's topical address in which he—through Betterton ("this the author bade me boldly say")—positioned his text in solid support of the king and, more importantly, his brother, the duke of York. Thus, each of Otway's original epilogues functions as a *post facto* lens, a textual prophylactic against misinterpretation. They recalibrated an elusive and problematic rebellion text into a royalist platform. The epilogue also offered to his Restoration audience exactly what modern readers like Mackenzie find missing: "a point of view from which the action is to be regarded." What follows is a brief reading of Otway's three epilogues.

III: "The Picture Mangler"

On 25 January 1682, while Charles II was attending the poet's benefit performance of another Exclusion play (Thomas D'Urfey's *The Roy-*

---

[4]Dryden was commissioned to write the prologues for all three productions, and although they have a general anti-Whig slant, they do not position the play nearly as aggressively as do Otway's epilogues.

alist) an anonymous vandal entered the Guildhall with a knife and slashed the picture of the duke of York, the king's brother and Catholic heir, who was the target of the Exclusion Bill and who, at the time, had been exiled to Scotland. The assault on the duke's image, occurring as it did in the heart of the city, raised violent detractions from the Catholic successor at exactly the time when the theatre was engaged in praising him. Nor did the symbolism of the assault go unnoticed. As described by *The London Gazette* the following day, the act "cannot be understood otherwise than an effect of Malice against his [Duke of York's] person" (1681/2, # 1690. See also Luttrell 1857, I, 170). Although a reward of £500 was advertised for a week for information leading to a conviction, the bounty went unclaimed and the culprit remained at large.

Otway chose this vandal's assault as a point of departure for his epilogue less than two weeks after the incident, on February 9, when *Venice Preserv'd* opened at the Duke's Theatre. But Otway used the occasion of the recent vandalism not to advertise dissent but to resurrect the by now old conflation of Whig and Cromwellian.[5] For Otway, the assault on the duke's image was an unholy act of Whig terrorism whose genealogy could be traced directly to the regicide of 1649:

> The rebel tribe, of which that vermin's one,
> Have now set forward, and their course begun;
> And while that prince's figure they deface,
> As they before had massacred his name,
> Durst their base fears but look him in the face,
> They'd use his person as they've us'd his fame;
> A face, in which such lineaments they read
> Of that great martyr's, whose rich blood they shed,
> That their rebellious hate they still retain,
> And in his son would murder him again.
>
> (ll. 25–35)

What I am concerned with here is how the dissent was sublimated into royal endorsement because how this process is played out in the epilogue is a replication in miniature of the interpretive strategies of the play itself. How Otway solved the sticky dilemma of transposing a re-

---

[5]The idea that the radicals of 1681 were replaying the rebellion of 1641 was a trope of Exclusion rhetoric. See, for example, D'Urfey's ballad *Advice to the City* (1682): "Remember ye Whigs what was formally done / Remember your mischiefs in forty and one."

bellion narrative into royalist encomium may be evidenced in miniature by slicing into his epilogue at its moment of greatest dissent.

Although an assault on the duke seems a curious point of attack to launch a campaign of loyalism, it is important because Otway uses the image of dissent in the city exactly as he uses the rebellion in the play: to lobby for the return of the exiled duke—both the Venetian duke and London's banished duke. Acknowledging the similarity of events in Venice and those in London concedes that the city does indeed contain a "rebel tribe," as evidenced in this latest assault at the Guildhall, and a tribe that poses a serious threat: "In his son would murder him again." Yet it also recognizes, like the play, that the city's rebellion is occasioned by an absent duke. The epilogue exploits the vandalism as an analog to the Venetian rebellion to elicit the audience's support for the return of the "injur'd Prince":

> With indignation then, let each brave heart
> Rouse, and unite to take his injur'd part;
> Till royal love and goodness call him home,
> And songs of triumph meet him as he come;
> Till heaven his honour, and our peace restore,
> And villains never wrong his virtue more.
> (ll. 36–41)

It is a nervy project to announce the physical danger to the duke and then petition for his recall. What makes Otway's rhetoric work is the recognition of the threat and his strategy of first pitting against this threat his own public endorsement of the duke's succession. Otway calls attention to both his authorship of the text and the epilogue's open declaration of loyalism as a public and claimed act that is set against the anonymous assault, and he invites his audience to concur. But to declare one's royalism is not an act without risk and therefore is an act that must be motivated by great personal integrity. Indeed, the epilogue contains a zealous display of such integrity that will "honor the truth" in spite of danger of personal revenge or private ambush:

> Poets in honour of the truth should write,
> With the same spirit brave men for it fight;
> and though against him causeless hatreds rise,
> and daily where he goes of late, he spies
> the scowls of sullen and revengeful eyes,
> 'Tis what he knows, with much contempt to bear,
> And serves a cause too good to let him fear:

He fears no poison from an incens'd drab,
No ruffian's five foot sword, nor rascal's stab;
Nor any other snares of mischief laid,
Not a Rose-alley cudgel-ambuscade.

(ll. 10–20)

The movement of the epilogue is designed in three parts: an invocation that announces the personal risks (referencing Dryden's Rose-
alley ambush) that accompany public declaration of royalism (ll. 7–20);
the central image of the anonymous and symbolic assault on the Duke
of York (ll. 25–35); and the subjunctive declaration of his own and his
public's support to take a stand against these rebels and call home the
banished Duke. The acknowledgement of danger—both personal danger and civic disruption—is an open concession to the power of the
opposition and an invocation to act loyally in the face of such opposition. The epilogue thus parallels the text of the play in dramatizing the
need of the royal presence in the face of local dissent.

IV: "You, Sir."

In the months that followed the play's initial run, the King did indeed recall his banished brother, and with the return of the Duke,
Otway's interest in application shifted. When the Duke of York returned to London in April of 1682, the Duke's Company revived
Otway's play for a special performance—part of a royalist celebration
that included a city feast at Merchant Taylors Hall. For this occasion
Otway designed a new epilogue. Now His Royal Highness at the Royal
Theatre found himself directly addressed "you Sir," and the address
occasioned an apostrophe to monarchy. In a sustained medical metaphor, to circumvent the return of '41 the "Great Physician" providen-
tially applies the Duke of York to cure the city's plague:

When too much Plenty, Luxury and Ease,
Had surfeited this Isle to a Disease;
When noisome Blaines did its best parts o'erspread,
And on the rest their dire infection shed;
Our Great Physician, who the Nature knew
Of the Distemper, and from whence it grew,
Fix't for Three Kingdoms quiet (Sir) on You:
He cast his searching Eyes o'er all the Frame,
And finding whence before one sickness came,
How once before our Mischiefs foster'd were,
Knew well Your Virtue, and apply'd You there:

Where so Your Goodness, so Your Justice sway'd,
You but appear'd and the wild Plague was stay'd.
                                        (ll. 1–13)

The rhetorical "application" of the first epilogue has now become lit-
eralized in the second, as the Duke himself is physically "apply'd," like
a poultice, to remedy the disease of rebellion that had run riot over the
state's body in his absence. Hovering behind the medicinal metaphor
is the symbolic act of "touching" as an intervention that both cures
the distemper and reaffirms the sanctity of the royal blood.[6] Narcissus
Luttrell tells us that in February of 1682 "the King hath lately toucht
for the evill" (Luttrell 1857, I, 162). It is an image that inscribes figuratively the divinity of the Duke as one capable of eradicating the ma-
lignancy of the "wild plague."

   Although politically timed to coincide with the Whig retreat, in reality the Duke's recall had little to do with reclaiming the city. But in
Otway's application (that is, play, prologue, and London) the Duke's
return was directly responsible for the Whig capitulation. Indeed, the
epilogue calls attention to the play just witnessed as a dramatization of
the return of the Duke to heal the troubled city. The play's second
epilogue thus represents the text's closest allegoric contact. At no point
do the times and the text meet quite so cleanly as with the Duke's
homecoming.

   The Duke of York was in many ways the ideal audience for *Venice
Preserv'd*. Though the power in Venice is lodged in a duke, this duke,
like James, was largely an absent duke. He enters the action quite late,
the last scene of act four, and seems, even at entrance, disoriented, re-
moved from the gravity of the Venetian political situation. The duke
needs exposition: "Anthony, Priuli, senators of Venice, / Speak; why are
we assembled here this night? / What have you to inform of us, concerns / The State of Venice, honour or its safety?" (4.2.1–4).[7] Quick to
judge, quick to torture, quick to mercy, quick to execute, Otway's duke
is an ambiguous figure, an accessory to the state and its absolute authority yet an untouchable suspended beyond the action until invoked in
times of crisis. Otway then surrounds this serviceable image with a

   [6]See, for example, the campaign to establish the legitimacy of James Scott, Duke of
Monmouth, Charles's eldest and illegitimate son, by a series of highly advertised incidents
of curing by touch. See *A Canto on the New Miracle Wrought by the Duke of Monmouth*
(London 1680).
   [7]All text quotations are from the Regents edition, Malcolm Kelsall, ed. (University of
Nebraska, 1969).

senatorial body that exercises no official power, registers no official voice, and performs no official role in the preserving of Venice. In the proceedings against the rebels, the Senate may utter collective or personal suggestions, but authority clearly resides in the duke. Yet noticeably, it is not the duke, but the senators who are the primary target of the rebellion. Indeed, in the rebel's venomous tirades against the state, the senators are repeatedly singled out:

> . . . But above all I charge you
> Shed blood enough; spare neither sex nor age,
> Name nor condition; if there live a senator
> After tomorrow, though the dullest rogue
> That e'er said nothing, we have lost our ends;
> If possible, let's kill the very name
> Of Senator, and bury it in blood.
>   (3.2.332–38)

In the general seizure of the city, along with St. Marks, the Secque, and the Procuralle, the ducal palace is also to be secured. Yet beyond one brief reference in the conspirator's general battle plan, the duke's name never arises. Vague as power is in Venice, it is nonetheless an odd *coup d'état* that takes so little account of the head of the state. Granted that Restoration plays routinely dislocate their narratives in extreme and often illogical ways to accommodate the sanctity of kingship (e.g., Tate's *King Lear*), it is a peculiar—though respectful—rebellion that annihilates the body of the state while preserving its head.

The rhetorical structuring of the two epilogues mirrors that of the play, whose central authority (the Duke) moves from absence to presence. In the first application, the Duke (of York) enters via his urged recall. In the second his presence is not only medicinal, healing the dissent, but paternal, describing an arc from exile to regeneration. The epilogue concludes by countering the symbolic castration of the picture mangler with an evocation of a royal birth that will ensure Stuart succession. It is, in the epilogue at least, an event praised by an "obedient land"—excepting, we take it, those who assaulted his image at Guildhall.

Again, like the first epilogue the second closes with a moment of extraordinary solidarity. Through the epilogue the playwright commandeers the playhouse, creating of his company and his audience a network of complicity in Jacobite support. It declares its own unambiguous Tory campaign while directing itself to any dissenters who might be in the house to beg his royal pardon. The presence of any dissent evoked by the original application has been effaced and the community now posited is unified in a "constant pledge to stand / of Caesar's love to an obedient Land." Even the evocation of "Caesar" repositions the Duke of York back within the mock-republican structure of the world of the play. It is to create of the duke an unassailable "Caesar" of a state modeled on Venice, represented by a puppet parliament of disempowered senators.

V: "Quo Warranto"

As we have seen, the function of the first epilogue was to use the theatre's captive community in the presence of His Majesty to lobby for the recall of the Duke of York. With the Duke's return, the second epilogue reestablished his claim as legitimate by his "touching" and curing the nation's dissent. The epilogue for the play's third production (again performed before Royalty on 31 May 1682, this time Her Highness Mary, James's very pregnant wife) picks up where the last one left off by envisioning not just the birth of an heir but a lasting and militant Stuart legacy based largely on the surrender of the city of London to the court of the Stuarts:

> Time have a care: bring home the hour of joy
> When some blest tongue proclaims a Royal Boy
> And when tis born, let Nature's hand be strong;
> Bless him with days of strength and make 'em long;
> Till charg'd with honors we behold him stand
> Three Kingdom's banners waiting his command,
> His Father's conquering sword within his Hand:
> Then the English Lions in the air advance
> And with them roaring music to the dance
> Carry a *Quo Warranto* into France.
>
> (ll. 17–26)

The *Quo Warranto* refers to the city of London's loss of privileges when Charles maneuvered the Lord Mayor to surrender its charter. The capitulation of the city—the dominant Whig stronghold that set itself against the king and court—is advanced as a model of foreign adversary. Internal resistance is sublimated into a national adversary, as the epilogue attempts to speak for the original dissidents, now reconciled to a larger national engagement.

France, however, the common adversary that would appease internal dissent, is itself synonymous with the two targets of the Whig party: Catholicism and absolutism. An anonymous ballad of 1680 vilifies Charles for having deep French interests: "who would reform this brutal nation / and bring French slavery in Fashion."[8] *French* and *popish* are interchangeable adjectives in Exclusion rhetoric, and both accusations are routinely leveled against Charles and his brother. A Catholic king with French ties will inevitably lead the country not into a War with the great rival but into a union based on the French model of Catholicism and absolutism.[9] Otway's strategy is to rewrite the implied association by expunging the Duke's Catholicism from the equation. This is Tory mythmaking at its boldest. With superlative disregard for the immediate history and personal memory of most of his audience, Otway calls for a nation of "English Lions" to rally under the yet unborn Catholic heir of a disputed Catholic heir and his "conquering [Catholic] sword" in a war against absolutism and Catholicism. It is a bizarre construction that requires a cultural amnesia to appease the insurgent anti-Catholicism that created and dominated the Exclusion crisis.

With each installment of the play, the longevity of the Stuart monarchy envisioned grows in size, in stability, and—noticeably—in militancy. Although the text itself remains unchanged, the application of the text undergoes enormous growth, moving from declaration of Otway's own public support at personal risk to the unabashed announcement of the national endorsement. Although the claims that Otway makes for fellow citizens' support of the Catholic heir apparent and his heir may seem hyperbolic, in terms of theatrical representation, his project of reapplying his text to the shifting political terrain over one spring is tantamount to a complete capitulation of the stage to the Jacobite cause. In the collapsed history of one play's "application," between the end of January and the end of May 1682, all trace of dissent evaporated. The three epilogues play out in miniature the elision of regicide and restoration as the image of the Duke of York moves through from mangling to regeneration.

[8] *Satire on Old Rowley*, vol. 2 of *Poems on Affairs of State* (New Haven: Yale University Press, 1965), 185. In another ballad Charles is made to say, "They pull'd my army down, with a hey, with a hey / and so they would my crown, with a ho / But to prevent that chance / I've sold it all to France / with a hey tronny nonny nonny no" (ibid., 177).

[9] The idea is articulated earliest in Marvell's *An Account of the Growth of Popery and Arbitrary Government* (1677) but continued throughout the polemics of the period. See, for example, Settle's *The Character of a Popish Successor, and What the Nation Can Expect of One* (1681) and its many rebuttals.

Works Cited

Boaden, James. 1825. *Memoirs of the Life of John Philip Kemble*. London: Longman, Hurst, Rees, Orme, Brown and Green.

Harth, Phillip. "Political Interpretations of *Venice Preserv'd*," *Modern Philology* 85 (1988): 345–62.

Luttrell, Narcissus. 1857. *A Brief Historical Relation of State Affairs from September 1678 to April 1714*. 6 vols. Oxford: Oxford University Press.

Nicoll, Allardyce. 1928. *A History of Restoration Drama*. Cambridge: Cambridge University Press.

Schless, H. H., ed. 1975. *Poems on Affairs of State: Augustan Satirical Verse, 1660–1714*. Vol. 3. New Haven: Yale University Press.

Sherburn, George, ed. 1956. *Correspondences of Alexander Pope*. Vol 4. Oxford: Clarendon Press.

Taylor, Aline Mackenzie. 1950. *Next to Shakespeare: Otway's* Venice Preserv'd *and* The Orphan. Durham: Duke University Press.

Wiley, Autrey, ed. 1940. *Rare Prologues and Epilogues*. London: George Allen and Unwin.

Federalist and Republican Theatre

in the 1790s

Steve Wilmer

*I*N THE LATE eighteenth century, following the establishment of a Federal Constitution and the election of George Washington as their first president, Americans began to write plays to record and eulogize the heroic acts of their compatriots during the War of Independence. This early form of nationalist theatre served to reinforce the legitimacy of the new nation-state. Rather than simply uniting the audience in proclaiming the virtues of their heritage, however, some of these plays were so partisan as to be divisive. This essay explores the phenomenon with special reference to two significant examples: John Burk's *Bunker-Hill; or, The Death of General Warren* (1797) and William Dunlap's *André* (1798), later revised as *The Glory of Columbia: Her Yeomanry* (1803).

Ostensibly, Burk's *Bunker-Hill*, performed in Boston and New York in 1797, celebrates American bravery in the War of Independence.[1] During the course of the play, Joseph Warren leaves the security of his own home and takes up arms against the British after the incidents at Lexington and Concord. A great battle scene takes place and General Warren dies defending Bunker Hill and the American cause. President John Adams, who attended a performance of the play in New York, was

---

[1]Certain leading theatre historians have categorized the play as simply patriotic. For example, Walter Meserve and Richard Moody both looked quite closely at Burk's play and failed to understand or preferred to ignore that the play was not simply patriotic but, more specifically, Jacobin and designed to redefine the values of the nation in opposition to the Federalist policies of the government. See Meserve 1977, 119–25 and Moody 1966, 61–69.

escorted out of the theatre afterwards by the actors and manager. When the actor who played Warren asked him what he thought of the performance, Adams replied tersely, "My friend, General Warren, was a scholar and a gentleman, but your author has made him a bully and a blackguard" (Clapp 1853, 55).

To understand Adams's strident reaction to what on the surface is a patriotic play, one must investigate the context in which the play was staged and the rhetorical techniques that were employed by the playwright. By the mid-1790s political factions had formed to support either Federalist or Republican policies. These factions grew out of the discussions over the Federal Constitution in the late 1780s with many politicians averse to a federal constitution that would transfer power from individual states to a centralized national government. In the 1790s, however, these opposing camps, which essentially divided over states' rights versus a strong national executive, were affected by the repercussions from the French Revolution and the subsequent war between Britain and France. The Federalists of the 1790s would align with the British and support a strong central government modeled on the British constitution; the Republicans would defend states' rights and the principles of the French Revolution. Adams, who had spent much of the 1780s in Paris and London as an American envoy, was a leading Federalist who believed in a bicameral legislature modeled on the House of Commons and the House of Lords. Referred to as "the Duke of Braintree" by his detractors, Adams published a *Defence of the Constitutions of Government of the United States of America* in 1787 that appeared dangerously aristocratic in tone, suggesting for example that the Senate should be composed of "the rich, the well-born and the able" (Adams 1954, 115). Adams tried to establish pompous ceremonies in Congress and the title "his Elective Majesty" for the president (see Curti 1964, 184).[2] Mercy Otis Warren, an embittered anti-Federalist, wrote in her *History of the Revolution* that Adams "might, by living long near the splendor of courts and courtiers, united with his own brightened prospects, have become so biased in his judgment as to think an hereditary monarchy the best Government for his native country" (quoted in Brown 1896, 226). Alexander Hamilton, another prominent Federalist who believed in a strong central government, formulated constitutional plans in the 1780s for an American president who would

---

[2]Adams managed to push through the Senate the title "His Highness the President of the United States of America and the Protector of the Rights of the Same," but it foundered in the House of Representatives. See Morison et al. 1980, I, 285.

serve for life and maintain an absolute veto over legislation (similar to a monarchy). In the late 1790s he hatched a plan to conquer the Spanish in Florida, Louisiana, and Mexico and to return like a Napoleonic hero to become First Citizen of America (McDonald 1982, 104 and Morison et al. 1980, 327).

The Federalists represented American shipping and mercantile interests and encouraged the creation of a loyal plutocracy and close links with Britain. They feared democratic influences from the French Revolution and worried that the accumulation of wealth and land in the hands of a small number of individuals would be threatened if the Republicans took power in America. Fisher Ames, one of the more outspoken Federalists, wrote of the dangers of the "barbarous, infuriated, loathsome mobs" of France (quoted in Curti 1964, 184).

By contrast, Thomas Jefferson, a leader of the Republicans, took a more democratic stance, supporting in 1791 Thomas Paine's pamphlet, "Rights of Man," which defended the French Revolution. Jefferson called the French Revolution "the most sacred cause that ever man was engaged in" (quoted in Morison et al. 1980, 301) and, in an introduction to the pamphlet, denounced "the political heresies" of John Adams (see Peterson 1978, 58). The political divisions in the country became more pronounced during the mid-1790s when the British and French went to war. The Federalists attracted northern merchants, ship owners, and professionals who depended on trade with Britain and who approved of Jay's Treaty with Britain in 1794 and the establishment of a national bank. The Republican movement gained the support of the planters in the South, the farmers in the West, and the laborers and artisans in the North and called for closer ties with France.[3] The Federalists under John Adams won the 1796 election, enforced Federalist principles of a strong central government, packed the judiciary with partisan supporters, and in 1798 introduced the Alien and Sedition Acts to stifle Republican dissent. Such Federalist measures were regarded as oppressive, however, and they led to a ground swell of support for Jefferson, who replaced Adams as president in 1800.

In the 1790s theatre was used as a public forum by both parties to

---

[3]Richard Butsch, 1995, in his valuable article, "American Theatre Riots and Class Relations, 1754–1849," simplifies the two parties as class divisions, i.e., rich employers and professionals against artisans. Although there is some truth in this, the alliances were more complex. For example, the rich planters of the South tended to favor the Republicans because they opposed a strong central government and because they feared having to repay their debts to Britain.

expound their respective ideological positions. The theatre in Boston, where John Burk first produced his play about Bunker Hill, was particularly affected by political divisions. Theatre in Boston had been outlawed since 1752, but from 1792 actors began to perform in spite of the law. In 1794 Federalist shareholders built the Federal Street Theatre and, in order to attract a large audience, tried to cater to all tastes. As party divisions became more acrimonious, however, politics began to disrupt the performances. As in other theatres, the orchestra of the Federal Street Theatre was often asked to play popular songs at the start of an evening's entertainment. In the 1790s this practice became an opportunity for partisan songs appealing to one faction or another. In other theatres, such as those in Philadelphia, a similar practice sometimes had led to riots, and now at the Federal Theatre, this display of party loyalties became unruly (Clapp 1853, 22–23).[4] In 1795 the manager wrote a poetic address to the audience (which he never gave but which was later published) asking them to leave their politics at home:

Let mirth within these walls your souls employ,
Like brothers worship at this shrine of joy;
Let Feds and Antis to our temples come,
And all unite firm *Federalists in Fun;*
Let austere politics one hour flee,
And join in free *Democracy of glee!*
                    (quoted in Clapp 1853, 26)

A rival theatre called the Haymarket was built in 1796 with financial help from Republicans, and the two theatres developed respective partisan followings. The shareholders of the Federal Street Theatre, members of the Boston elite, took pride in personally covering the expenses of the theatre and ensuring capacity audiences. If they were not able to sell all the tickets, shareholders would give remaining tickets away on condition that recipients refuse to patronize the rival Haymarket Theatre (Burk 1891, 12; Clapp 1853, 50–51). The manager was encouraged to present pieces that would annoy Republicans, and the actors (who in most cases were from England) were encouraged to make jokes at the expense of France, with whom England was at war. Such

---

[4]According to theatre historian Arthur Quinn, "In 1798 the Chestnut Street Theatre was nightly a scene of rivalry between the two parties as to which could stir up more enthusiasm for its favorites" (1923, 130 n. 1). William Dunlap also refers to a disturbance in the New York theatre when the orchestra leader was not "ready with a popular air when called upon" by Republicans (1833, I, 210).

politically motivated actions often led to serious disturbances in the theatre, such as one during the run of *Poor Soldier*. According to "Dramatic Reminiscences": "The anti-federal, (or, as it was then called, the Jacobin) party, were so extremely sensitive, that they took great offence at the representation of the *Poor Soldier*—pretending that the character of Bagatelle was a libel on the character of the whole French nation. They were encouraged in this, by the French consul, then residing in Boston. A pretty smart quarrel was excited between him and the editor of the *Boston Gazette;* and the controversy, at last, became so bitter, that a mob, on one occasion, attempted to stop the performance of this farce, and did considerable damage to the benches, doors, and windows of the theatre" (*New England Magazine* 1832, 38–39).[5] Subsequently the manager had to cut the character of Bagatelle from the play (Hornblow 1919, I, 237).[6]

Later, during a performance of the comic-opera *Lock and Key,* a similar row occurred because of a song that praised the heroism of the English in a battle with the French. According to William Clapp, "The song was encored, and repeated with general applause and partial hisses, which by the lively jealousies of party spirit, then dominant, was construed into mutual insult. The first night was only a first rehearsal; the second night more clamor occurred, and on the third night the heroes of the sock became passive spectators and the audience the principal actors, and presented a medley entertainment in its finished state, so far as disorder can approximate to perfection. The attempt to stop the song, was ineffectual; for the friends of the theatre prevailed" (1853, 74–75).

The Haymarket Theatre, on the other hand, presented works that appealed to a Republican clientele. During the period that the theatre was under construction, it became clear that the people pledging money for its development expected a different approach from that of the Federal Street Theatre.[7] The Federal Street Theatre was regarded as cater-

---

[5]It appears that, rather than the *Boston Gazette,* the author was referring to the *Columbia Centinel,* which printed a letter from the French consul Mozard complaining about an article in the newspaper that had defamed France. The editor printed a caustic reply to the consul as well as a series of letters, written under the pseudonym of Leonidas, attacking France. (See *Columbia Centinel* from April 19 until the end of May 1797).

[6]The rivalry between the theatres continued until the Federal Street Theatre burned down in 1798 (See Clapp 1881, IV, 363–64).

[7]The manager of the Haymarket Theatre, according to historian William Clapp, "availed himself of the strong political antagonism which prevailed between the Federalists and so-called jacobins to induce the latter to believe that the old theatre was managed with a view of promoting political animosities" (Clapp 1881, IV, 363). It may have been

ing to the Boston elite and as looking askance not only at the French but also at local tradesmen and artisans. Many of the workmen involved in building the Haymarket Theatre gave their services for free in return for becoming shareholders and obtaining free tickets. According to William Clapp, "The Boston mechanics were not partial to the Federal Street, and favored the project . . . and those who were not able to pay the money, also subscribed for shares, and paid in labor, furnishing the material for constructing the building" (1853, 36–37). A "tradesman" writing to the editor of the *Boston Gazette* on 9 May 1796 confirmed the expectations of certain members of the Republican community that the theatre would cater to common people and accused the patrons of the Federal Theatre of personal abuse and immorality: "I am highly pleased with the prospect of having a new Theatre established upon a cheap and liberal plan, that we Tradesmen can go with our families and partake of a rational and pleasing amusement for a little money, and not be hunched up by *one* [*sic*], and the nose of another Aristocrat turned up at us, because we are Tradesmen. The present theatre is an imposition on the Town—it is only a 'School of Scandal' and *Aristocracy*, and of late the Slip Galleries are no better than Brothels (*Boston Gazette*, 9 May 1796, n.p.).

While the Haymarket was still in its first season, the manager of the competing Federal Street Theatre hinted at the class divisions that separated the theatres, declaring that the "prevailing Jacobin spirit in the lower ranks" prevented the Federal Street Theatre from gaining a larger audience. After the first week of competition, the Federal Street Theatre lowered its prices for the pit and gallery seats in order to maintain its audience, but competition from the new theatre diminished attendance noticeably. The Federal Street Theatre manager complained: "They have brought out a new piece, called *Bunker's Hill,* a tragedy, the most execrable of the Grub Street kind—but from its locality in title, the burning of Charlestown and *peppering* the *British* (which are superadded to the tragedy in pantomime), to the utter disgrace of Boston theatricals, has brought them *full houses*" (Dunlap 1833, I, 312).

The playwright, John Burk, was a colorful figure. The son of a Protestant school teacher from County Cork in Ireland and said to be related to the statesman Edmund Burke, he attended Trinity College, Dublin in 1792, where he was accused of republicanism and deism (*Polar Star*

---

partly to appeal to Republican tastes that Powell hired French and Irish and not just English actors for his company. The actor who played General Warren, for example, was an Irishman.

and Daily Advertiser 26 October 1796, n.p.). He became involved in the Irish rebellion (which was aided by the French) to overthrow British rule in Ireland and, according to him, "attempted by every means in [my] power to effect [Ireland's] emancipation" (*Polar Star and Daily Advertiser* 9 January 1797, n.p.). After attempting to rescue a rebel from execution, Burk was chased by the police through the city; he ducked into a shop where he was given women's clothes by a young woman and, thus disguised, took the next boat to America (Burk 1891, 1). He held strong Republican views, which he expressed as a newspaper editor first in Boston and later in New York. He was arrested in 1798 under the Sedition Act along with other editors of Republican newspapers.[8] He was killed in a duel with a Frenchman in 1808 when he was in his early thirties, but he had already written several plays, a history of the Irish rebellion, and a three-volume history of Virginia.

Burk's adherence to Republican principles is clearly conveyed in *Bunker-Hill,* which he dedicated to Aaron Burr (a leading Republican who helped Burk escape the charges of sedition in 1798 and who would become vice president in 1801 under Jefferson). The rhetorical strategies he employed made the play recognizable as Republican to the audience. He depicted General Warren, the hero of the melodramatic tragedy, as an altruistic patriot who does not demand a privileged social position but wants to do whatever he can to help his countrymen. Called by the patriots to serve in the army, Warren offers to act in any capacity: "Yes, I will go; / And share with them the hardships of the war: / Whether as private, or as leader rang'd; / My post is honor and my country's good" (Burk 1891, 41). When the battle commences he stands in the front lines with his men rather than asserting the usual privilege of a commanding officer to remain behind the lines and away from the danger of combat. As his men retreat, he remains to supervise their exodus: "I will not stir till every soul be safe, / Who fought with me this day" (74). As he is ensuring their safe retreat, however, he is mortally wounded by a British sniper.

Within the political context of the day, it was clearly a Republican strategy to emphasize the role of Britain as adversary. A spectacular bat-

---

[8]Burk claimed impartiality for his *Polar Star and Daily Advertiser,* but it was clearly pro-French and anti-British and anti-monarchist. During the 1796 election campaign between Adams and Jefferson, Burk feigned impartiality but hinted at his support for Jefferson. *The Time-Piece,* which he edited in 1798, was much more outspoken about its Republican sympathies. (See, e.g., *The Time-Piece,* June–July 1798.)

tle scene, lasting approximately fifteen minutes, was mounted in the theatre to depict the gallant struggle by the American patriots against the British military (Dunlap 1833, I, 314). In a letter to the manager of the John Street Theatre in New York requesting another production of the play, Burk described the effects in the Boston production:

> The hill is raised gradually by boards extended from the stage to a bench. Three men should walk abreast on it, and the side where the English march up should for the most part be turned towards the wings; on our hill there was room for eighteen or twenty men, and they were concealed by a board painted mud color, and having two cannon painted on it— which board was three feet and a half high. The English marched in two divisions from one extremity of the stage, where they ranged, after coming from the wings, when they come to the foot of the hill. The Americans fire—the English fire—six or seven of your men should be taught to fall—the fire should be frequent for some minutes. The English retire to the front of the stage—second line of English advance from the wing near the hill—firing commences—they are again beaten back— windows on the stage should be open to let out the smoke. All the English make the attack and mount the hill. After a brisk fire, the Americans leave works and meet them. Here is room for effect, if the scuffle be nicely managed. Sometimes the English falling back, sometimes the American—two or three Englishmen rolling down the hill. A square piece about nine feet high and five wide, having some houses and a meeting-house painted on fire, with flame and smoke issuing from it, should be raised two feet distance from the horizon scene at the back of your stage, the windows and doors cut out for transparencies—in a word, it should have the appearance of a town on fire. (quoted in Dunlap 1833, I, 313)

In addition to depicting the Americans making a heroic stand against the English military, Burk emphasized the difference between American values and British values. In a scene in which a British officer tries to negotiate a truce with Warren and offers him a pardon, Burk used the situation as an opportunity to attack British justice. (Being a fugitive from British justice himself, Burk clearly had a vested interest in the subject.) Warren asks the officer,

> What are your boasted English laws to us,
> Or any laws, which sanctify injustice?
> Is it an English law, to rob the weak,
> To wring his pittance from the shiv'ring poor,
> To levy taxes like a Russian czar . . .
>
> (Burk 1891, 60)

Burk, however, signaled to the audience not simply nationalist values but more specifically Republican values. Earlier in the play Warren asserts the political rights of all individuals: "Those sacred rights, which nature had design'd / Alike, for all the children of this earth" (Burk 1891, 39). Echoing the rhetoric of the day, which identified the Federalists as monarchists and the Republicans as democrats, Burk used Warren to denounce monarchy as a political system. Warren asks, "What are kings? / Kings form a horrid junto of conspiracy, / A Catilinian compact, 'gainst the lives, / The rights, the peace, the freedom of the world" (Burk 1891, 61). Near the end of the play, in his dying words, Warren calls for an end to aristocratic titles in the new nation:

> O might I look into the womb of time
> And see my country's future destiny:
> Cou'd I but see her proud democracy,
> Founded on equal laws, and stript entire,
> Of those unnatural titles, and those names
> Of *King*, of *Count*, of *Stadtholder*, and *Duke*,
> Which, with *degrading awe*, possess the world.
> (Burk 1891, 79)

Warren's funeral, performed with pomp and ceremony, again employed rhetorical emblems. Burk's stage directions emphasize the partisan nature of the scene with Republican slogans being carried beside Warren's coffin: "THE RIGHTS OF MAN," "LIBERTY AND EQUALITY," "HATRED TO ROYALTY" (Burk 1891, 81). Such sentiments were reminiscent as much of the French as the American Revolution. The play ends with a panegyric in which "two virgins" sing of Warren's heroism and call for the emotional involvement of the audience:

> You sons and daughters of the land,
> From *all* his virtues tears demand,
> You soldiers and you farmers, hear
> Your hero's glories with a tear.
> And you of Boston, who have seen
> Oft in your streets his warlike mien,
> Join in the general song of grief,
> Which freedom gives to freedom's chief.
> (Burk 1891, 82)

By referring to "farmers and soldiers" in the funeral audience (which by extension included the theatre audience), Burk again employed a rhetorical device to appeal to the common people as against the Boston elite.

The play, however, was not only partisan. By setting the play during the War of Independence, Burk subsumed his partisan politics within a nationalist frame in order to appeal to a wide audience. Furthermore, by selecting a local Massachusetts hero, he was assured the interest of a local audience. Although the Republican slogans carried at Warren's funeral were in a sense anachronistic (as they were associated with the French Revolution more than a decade after Warren's death) and certainly offensive to the ardent Federalists, their effect was muted by the emotional moment of mourning for a national hero. By placing the rhetoric of the Jeffersonian party of the 1790s within the era of the Revolutionary War, Burk sought to legitimize Republican principles as founding values of the nation-state.

Today one might view these party politics as petty and of minor importance, but they were not simply squabbles among individuals ambitious for power. The issues involved important ideological differences over the direction that the country would take. At the time it seemed quite possible that the United States might become a monarchy, or at least an oligarchy, with repressive legislative initiatives such as the Sedition Act to stifle opposition. Adams, for example, told friends in the early 1790s that he thought monarchy was inevitable for the United States. To Benjamin Rush he wrote that monarchy and aristocracy were "the only institutions that can possibly preserve the laws and liberties of the people, and I am clear that Americans must resort to them as an asylum against discord, seditions and civil war, and that at no very distant period of time" (quoted in Peterson 1978, 54–55). Jefferson recalled the period of the 1790s as involving "contests of principle between the advocates of republican and those of kingly government" (quoted in Banning 1978, 13). It was important therefore for the Republicans not simply to appeal to a narrow following but to gain control of the majority and win the next election in order to thwart Federalist policies. Furthermore, the political figures of the day did not see their parties as permanent oppositional forces in the political system as today but as temporary divisions that would ultimately reunite the nation under their own banner. In his letter to the New York theatre, Burk indicated that the play had succeeded in appealing not only to the gallery and pit but to all sections of the audience: "It was played seven nights successively, and on the last night was received with the same enthusiasm as on the first—it revived old scenes, and united all parts of the house. Mr. Powell [the manager] intends it for a stock play, and it will be represented on all festivals—such as 4th July, 19th June [the anniversary of the battle of Bunker Hill], etc. It will be played here in a few nights again, immediately after *Columbus*. . . . There will no doubt be some who will call in question your prudence in getting up this piece, as being not in favour of England. Those are blockheads, and know not the public opinion of America. Boston is as much divided as New York—party was forgotten in the representation of it" (quoted in Dunlap 1833, I, 313–14).

The play successfully operated on two rhetorical levels simultaneously. It served as a partisan comment to bolster the Republican cause and as a patriotic reminiscence that could unite the audience. Although it was a Federalist newspaper, the *Columbia Centinel* of 22 February 1797 praised the play after its sensational first night "to a larger and more respectable auditory than perhaps was ever contained in any other theatre on the continent. The numbers present on this occasion could only be determined by calculating the dimensions of the house; for there appeared to be hardly a nook or corner in it unoccupied." The critic commented on the united response of the audience, which had eagerly awaited the play because of its title: "Approbation was universal and instantaneous—not merely the calm, deliberate sanction of judgment, it was expressed in a language of passion in a high degree of incitement— a language in which box, pit and gallery were perfectly concordant. Since the memorable event on which the plot of the piece is founded, we presume there has seldom been so unaffected an expression of the genuine American spirit of '75. For a moment the audience seemed lost in the fiction, and to have imagined the flames of Charlestown, and the death of WARREN, something more than a delusive description of events that had passed."

In a spirit of patriotism, the reviewer concluded: "On the whole, it must be confessed, that *Bunker-Hill* is not less unrivalled as a play, than it has been in reality unequalled in the history of military glory." After a relatively long run of four performances with full houses, the paper predicted on 1 March 1797 that the play could run much longer with equal success and urged everyone to see it, suggesting it might be unpatriotic not to do so: "The uncommon success attending the Bunker-Hill tragedy exceeds the expectations of the most sanguine. Four crowded houses have witnessed, by the loudest plaudits, to its excellence; and if given out for four times more will still fill the house. Not to have seen Bunker Hill tragedy will fix on the delinquent a want of taste, and a deficiency of patriotism." The play became a rallying point not only for Republicans but for all Americans, and it could and would be performed for decades all over New England on national occasions such as the fourth of July.[9]

When the play was produced in New York in 1797, theatre administrator and playwright William Dunlap revealed his own prejudices by describing it as "deplorable" and referring to the audiences who came to see it as "mere rabble," unlike "the first and most respectable of our people" who attended a rival performance by leading English actors (Dunlap 1931, I, 144; also Dunlap 1833, I, 313). Dunlap was a Federalist whose father served with the British army in the French and Indian War and settled in Perth Amboy, New Jersey, where Dunlap was born. During the War of Independence, the Dunlaps remained loyal to the Crown and moved to New York where William Dunlap saw numerous plays presented by the British military who were occupying the city. After the war William Dunlap studied to be an artist in England and returned to New York to work in the theatre as a playwright and theatre manager, helping to run the John Street Theatre and then the Park Theatre. One of his early dramatic efforts, an interlude based on O'Keefe's *Poor Soldier,* called *Darby's Return* (1789), suggested his Federalist leanings, with the eponymous hero mocking the French revolution in such lines as, "I went to France. I always did love quiet, / And there I got in the middle of a riot" (quoted in Coad 1917, 142).[10]

By the mid-1790s the New York theatre was experiencing popular reactions from its audiences similar to those occurring in the Boston theatre. Dunlap reports an incident in 1794 when the advertising for *Tammany* made use of a "ruse . . . to collect an audience for the support of the piece, by circulating a report that a party had been made up to hiss it." Dunlap quotes the *Daily Advertiser* as describing "the audience assembled as made up of 'the poorer class of mechanics and clerks,' and

---

[9]The play continued to be performed successfully in New York and elsewhere on through the Jacksonian era. It was printed in 1797 and reprinted in 1808 and 1817. Charles Blake attested to the ongoing success of the play through the first half of the nineteenth century. The play, he wrote, "has proved very remunerative to the theatrical treasury in Boston. It was very well received here [in Providence when it was first produced] and the company then left town, to produce it in Newport. Miserable as the play was it survived many dramas superior to it in every respect, and is now sometimes brought out on the Fourth of July in New England cities for the benefit of visitors from the rural districts" (quoted in Burk 1891, 12).

[10]Although the author admitted in the preface to the play that it was a slight piece, it was printed many times apparently with the encouragement of Dunlap's friends (see Dunlap 1931, I, 160).

of bankrupts who ought to 'be content with the mischief they had already done, and who might be much better employed than in disturbing a theatre' " (1833, I, 209–10). He also recorded that when the actor Hodgkinson entered the stage as Captain Flash in *Miss in Her Teens* dressed in an English military uniform, he

> was hissed and called upon by the French party to take it off. He came forward, and, to the satisfaction of the French partisans, said he represented a coward and a bully. Unfortunately, this was running on Charybdis to avoid Scylla, and the English partisans threatened vengeance on the actor. Always ready to speak or to write, Hodgkinson came out in *The Daily Advertiser,* and, to satisfy all parties, professed to give the exact words of his "address" made on compulsion, as follows;—"Sir, the character I am going to portray is a bully and a coward, and however you may choose to quarrel with a redcoat, you would probably be a great deal more offended had I improperly disgraced the uniform of this or any other country, by wearing it on the back of a poltroon." Here it is to be observed, he admits that to wear the uniform of any country on the back of such a character was to disgrace it, and *he had worn* an English uniform. He goes on to say, that he was placed before the audience to represent an English officer, and should have deserved reprobation if he had worn an American or French uniform. This statement, under the signature of Verax, only made matters worse with the actor's countrymen, and other adherents of Old England. (1833, I, 214–15)

In 1797, when Burk's *Bunker-Hill* was staged, Dunlap was working on a Federalist novel tentatively called *Anti-Jacobin* (which was never finished) and helping to run the John Street Theatre. He also wrote a satirical afterpiece, "Fractura Minimi Digiti," about a French surgeon living in New York. The insulted Frenchman failed to appreciate Dunlap's humor and assaulted him as he came out of church (Coad 49–50). On a visit to Boston to oversee a theatre company, Dunlap befriended ardent Federalists and described the atmosphere in a manner recalling scenes oddly transformed from the period prior to the American Revolution: "Much political conversation, high federalists, much exasperated against the French. . . . [Samuel] Cooper gave me an account of the party conflicts of the Town in which he was the Federal Champion, cutting down french flags & liberty poles at the risque of his life, fighting mobs &c &c and writing down Governor [Samuel] Adams in the News papers" (1931, I, 175).

Dunlap's most notable play at this time, *André* (1798), was a tragedy about the British spy John André, who colluded with Benedict Arnold in an attempt to capture the American fort at West Point. Although tackling a historical subject that could have displayed "gung-ho" American patriotism, Dunlap's Federalist sympathies played a strong part in his writing, with the subtext of the play calling for reconciliation between England and America rather than (as in *Bunker-Hill*) replaying past grievances. The rhetoric of *André* suggests that there were errors on both sides and that the British suffered as well as the Americans. Instead of denouncing the treachery of Arnold and André and celebrating the American discovery of their plot, Dunlap concentrated on the honorable character of André and his misfortune in being hung for espionage. Several characters visit General Washington to plead for mercy to no avail, and the play ends as André goes to the gallows. André is depicted as a mistreated victim of war, and Washington appears somewhat hard-hearted in his refusal to commute the death sentence. The most surprising character in the play is a passionate American officer and friend of André named Bland, who threatens to change sides and fight for Britain if he cannot obtain André's pardon. In pleading with General Washington, Bland argues: "Yet, let not censure fall on André. / O, there are Englishmen as brave, as good, / As ever land on earth might call its own; / And gallant André is among the best!" (Dunlap [1798] 1953, 96). When Washington refuses to pardon André, Bland removes the American cockade off his helmet and throws it on the ground with the words, "Thus from my helm / I tear what once I proudly thought, the badge / Of virtuous fellowship."

Clearly Dunlap misjudged the public's sentiments, for on opening night the audience reacted to this scene with hisses. The Republican newspaper *Argus* attacked the play, and mass action was threatened at the second performance. Observing in his diary, "I am told that the people are so offended at the Cockade business as to threaten to hiss off the play tonight" (I, 237), Dunlap rewrote the act to make it less controversial with Bland in a subsequent scene apologizing for his actions, praising Washington, and graciously retrieving the cockade. Nevertheless, box office receipts dropped from $800 on the first night to $271 and $329 on the last two nights, and the play was removed from the repertory (Coad 62).

Not until the Jeffersonian era did the play become popular. In 1803, following Jefferson's election and the demise of Federalism, Dunlap rewrote it using Republican rhetorical devices and renamed it *The Glory of Columbia: Her Yeomanry*. He introduced new scenes and characters, emphasized the virtuous actions of American common soldiers, and reduced André's status from martyr and victim to a man responsible for his own fate. Rather than the honorable gentleman of the earlier work, André is shown ignobly taking part in espionage activities with Benedict Arnold and trying to bribe American soldiers when they capture him.

Instead of ending the play with André's noble march to his death, Dunlap replaced the execution scene with a scene at the battle of Yorktown depicting General Washington and the common American soldiers heroically encircling the British and winning the war. Dunlap dropped the cockade incident, and although there remained an underlying suggestion of reconciliation between the English and the Americans, he gave the French a prominent part in the action. In *André* the French did not appear as characters and were indirectly criticized with lines such as M'Donald's rhetorical question: "Are other nations in that happy state, / That, having broke Coercion's iron yoke, / They can submit to Order's gentle voice, / And walk on earth self-ruled?" (Dunlap [1798] 1953, 90). In *The Glory of Columbia,* however, Dunlap allowed the French general Rochambeau and the French common soldiers such prominence in the final scene as to credit them with partial responsibility for the final victory. Dunlap also emulated Burk's spectacular battle effects. The advance publicity, appearing in the *New York Evening Post,* 3 July 1803, described what audiences could expect to see:

> A View of Yorktown. With the British lines, and the lines of the besiegers. Nearer the audience are the advanced battalions of the besieged. Cannonading commences from the Americans upon the town, which is returned. Shells thrown into the town. Explosion of a powder magazine. The French troops advance towards the most distant of the advanced batteries; the battalion begins to cannonade, but is carried at the bayonets point. (*This is done by artificial figures in perspective.*) While this is yet doing, the nearest battalion begins to cannonade, and the American Infantry rushing to the charge, they attack and carry it with fixed bayonets. (*This is done by boys completely equip'd and of a size to correspond in perspective with the machinery and the scenery.*) The British are seen asking quarter, which is given (quoted in Coad, 74–75).

The hero of the piece is no longer André but the common American soldier. One of the new characters, David Williams, uses his intuition and common sense to frustrate Arnold's and André's devious actions. Moreover, he displays a virtuous sense of responsibility in looking after the welfare of his sister and his family farm at the same time he carries on his duties as a soldier. Dunlap transformed his tragedy about a maligned English officer and gentleman into a eulogy on the virtuous American common soldier. As such it became a popular success and was revived for many years to come.

In conclusion, the new American plays of the 1790s often used recent American history for ideological reasons. Major theatre historians such as Walter Meserve and Richard Moody have categorized the work of such writers as Burk and Dunlap as patriotic, but it is important to distinguish the underlying rhetoric of these plays and to recognize their partisan nature in order to understand their effect on the audiences of the period.

Works Cited

Adams, John. [1787] 1954. *The Political Writings of John Adams,* ed. George A. Peek, Jr. Indianapolis: Bobbs-Merrill Company, Inc.

Banning, Lance. 1978. *The Jeffersonian Persuasion.* Ithaca: Cornell University Press.

Boston Gazette, May 1796.

Brown, Alice. 1896. *Mercy Warren.* New York: Charles Scribner's Sons.

Burk, John. 1891. *Bunker-Hill; or, The Death of General Warren.* New York: Publications of the Dunlap Society, no. 15.

Butsch, Richard. 1995. "American Theatre Riots and Class Relations, 1754–1849." *Theatre Annual* 48:41–59.

Clapp, William W. 1853. *A Record of the Boston Stage.* Boston: James Munroe and Company.

———. 1881. "The Drama in Boston." In *The Memorial History of Boston,* Vol. 4, ed. Justin Winsor, 357–82. Boston: J. R. Osgood and Company.

Coad, Oral S. 1917. *William Dunlap.* New York: Dunlap Society.

Columbia Centinel. 1797 (February, March, April, May).

Curti, Merle. 1964. *The Growth of American Thought.* New York: Harper and Row.

Dunlap, William. 1833. *History of the American Theatre.* London: Richard Bentley.

———. 1931. *The Diary of William Dunlap,* ed. Dorothy C. Barck. New York: The New York Historical Society.

———. [1798] 1953. *André.* In *Representative American Plays,* ed. A. H. Quinn. New York: Appleton-Century-Crofts.

———. [1803] 1966. *The Glory of Columbia: Her Yeomanry.* In *Dramas from the American Theatre,* ed. Richard Moody. Bloomington: Indiana University Press.

Hornblow, Arthur. 1919. *A History of Theatre in America.* Philadelphia: Lippincott Company.

McDonald, Forrest. 1982. *Alexander Hamilton.* New York: W. W. Norton and Co.

Meserve, Walter. 1977. *An Emerging Entertainment: The Drama of the American People to 1828.* Bloomington: Indiana University Press.

Moody, Richard, ed. 1966. *Dramas from the American Theatre.* Bloomington: Indiana University Press.

Morison, Samuel Eliot, Henry Steele Commager, and William E. Leuchtenburg. 1980. *The Growth of the American Republic.* Oxford: Oxford University Press.

New England Magazine (1832).

Peterson, Merrill D. 1978. *Adams and Jefferson: A Revolutionary Dialogue.* Oxford: Oxford University Press.
Polar Star and Daily Advertiser (Boston) 1796–97.
Quinn, Arthur. 1923. *History of the American Drama from the Beginning to the Civil War.* New York: Appleton-Century-Crofts.
The Time Piece (New York) June–July, 1798.

Uncle Tom's Cabin and the

Rhetoric of Gradualism

Charles Wilbanks

*I*N HER RECENT work on Puritan rhetorical form, Gladys Sherman Lewis writes that "Harriet Beecher Stowe caused social change with her literary strategies. The dynamics between the message, messenger, and audience in *Uncle Tom's Cabin* demonstrate her methodology with her vision, voice, and readers to implement the public morality for America that she desired" (1994, 1). Stowe's classic clearly is a literary effort that plunged headlong into the political debate raging at the time of its writing. The rhetorical impact of the novel was considerable. Lewis writes of *Uncle Tom's Cabin:* "The book performs as one huge sermon; in both rhetoric and style, it stands alongside the Puritan sermons [that] Eugene White, Harry Stout, Phyllis Jones, Nicholas Jones, and other critics analyze" (3–4). During the fourteen decades since the work first appeared, it has been analyzed from a number of rhetorical and political perspectives, including "feminist, Marxist, religionist, archetypist, [and] Freudian" (2).

Fundamentally, *Uncle Tom's Cabin* is an antislavery manifesto. It is first and foremost a screaming indictment of slavery written with passion and emotion. Although the book heightened passions in both the North and the South, the message was one that I believe was intended to be heard by the abolitionist North. Obviously, the dramatizations that followed were intended to be performed before northern audiences. Abraham Lincoln has been quoted as saying upon meeting Harriet Beecher Stowe, "So this is the little woman who wrote the book that started this big war" (Stowe, 180–81). Lincoln's dark jest underscores the widespread controversy inspired by the novel and the emotional portraits Stowe painted of its characters. Whatever impact the work had on the actual practice of slavery or the onset of the war, its impact within the antislavery movement was monumental.

Historically, abolitionists have been seen monolithically. Until recently, political divisions caused by the slavery question have been seen by historians as being between the proslavery South and the antislavery North. For a number of reasons, such a view is a simplistic distortion of the antebellum political landscape. Cleavages *within* the antislavery movement were nearly as deep as those between the North and the South. This essay seeks to illustrate the ways in which Stowe represented a brand of abolitionism philosophically at odds with that of a significant segment of the movement.

Almost immediately after the appearance of the novel, various dramatizations began touring the North. These dramatizations, created to capitalize on the celebrity of the novel, created in turn much of the political reaction that further fueled the novel's popularity. Because these dramatizations tapped the immediacy of the stage before their audiences, the rhetorical aspects of the work can more easily be seen. The most popular adaptation was George L. Aiken's, whose dramatization serves as the source of the text references in this essay.

The Antislavery Divisions

Ernest Bormann has written in *The Force of Fantasy* that abolitionists were of two camps: evangelists and secularists (1985, 23). Ronald G. Walters identifies the divisions as primarily between Garrisonians and evangelical protestants (1976, 9). According to Walters, the Garrisonians were more violent in their rhetoric than the evangelicals (9).

Some believe that the divisions within the movement were more complex than Bormann and Walters indicate. Smith and Windes, for example, suggest that dividing abolitionists into just two groups ignores the complexities of the movement (1993, 45). Elsewhere, they suggest that a better way to analyze abolitionist rhetoric is through a "terministic" approach or the examination of the uses of shared language (1995, 303).

The most important division, however, cannot be identified in any of the above analyses. The dispute that created the largest and most fundamental schism was between the gradualists and those who insisted on the immediate abolition of slavery. The philosophical differences separating these two groups were immense. Garrisonians insisted on moral purification; gradualists sought a more pragmatic solution. The dispute thus pitted those who viewed slavery only as a national sin to be cleansed against those who viewed slavery as primarily a political problem. A political dispute might be resolved through compromise. The cleansing of sin allows no compromise.

Stowe as a Gradual Abolitionist

An analysis of *Uncle Tom's Cabin* reveals clearly that Harriet Beecher Stowe favored gradualism. Her treatment of her characters makes such a conclusion undeniable. Stowe was not just promoting abolition; she was advocating a particular approach to the problem that was not shared by everyone in the movement. The following analysis centers on two pairs of characters: Uncle Tom and Eva on the one hand, Topsy and Miss Ophelia on the other. The message of gradualism is clearly promoted through the treatment of these characters.

Harriet Beecher Stowe came by her antislavery views naturally. Her father, Lyman Beecher, was an ardent abolitionist as was her older sister Catharine. In 1837 Catharine Beecher published *An Essay on Slavery and Abolition*. The essay was written largely in response not to the proslavery propagandists of the day but to Angelina Grimké, another abolitionist. Grimké, a protégée of the militant William Lloyd Garrison and a supporter of the American Anti-slavery Society, had just published *An Appeal to the Christian Women of the South*. In it she called for the immediate abolition of slavery and called on Christian women in particular to speak out against what she called the sin of slavery. Although also believing slavery to be a sin, Beecher took issue with a variety of positions that Grimké had promulgated in her *Appeal*. Foremost among her counterarguments was the sheer inexpediency of Grimké's demand. Beecher insisted that it seemed "inexpedient for ladies of the non-slave-holding states to unite themselves in Abolition societies" (6). Beecher's complaint was really based on Grimké's insistence that the slave owners repent their sin and release their slaves at once. Beecher complained that such a message was more likely to increase passions in the South and make more difficult the process of emancipation. Although she agreed that slave owners in some sense "ought" immediately to release their slaves, they simply could not. She explained that "a slaveholder cannot legally emancipate his slaves, without throwing them into worse bondage, he is bound to use all his influence to alter those laws, and in the meantime, to treat his slaves, as nearly as he can, as if they were free" (7).

Beecher believed that there was a more expedient path. In a passage that reflects the pragmatic lens through which Beecher saw the problem of slavery, she wrote: "The best way to make a person like a thing which is disagreeable is to try, in some way, to make it agreeable; and if a certain class of persons is the subject of unreasonable prejudice, the peaceful and Christian way of removing it would be to endeavor to render the unfortunate persons who compose this class [slaves], so useful, so humble and unassuming, so kind in their feelings, and so full of love and good works, that prejudice would be supplanted by complacency in their goodness and pity and sympathy for their disabilities" (26–27). This passage reflects the essence of the gradualist position. Beecher suggests that all parties, slave and slave owner have obligations to resolve the problem. She observes that those who call for immediate abolition, instead of enhancing the social "acceptability" of the slave, actually entrench opposition to abolition and excite the passions on both sides.

Beecher proposed that antislavery efforts should not be aimed at the slaveholder but at improving the slave so that slaveholders would *want* to change the system. To this reasoning the Garrisonians responded with outrage. Grimké was pointed in her response to Beecher on this issue: "So then, instead of convincing a person by sound argument and pointed rebuke that sin is *sin*, we are to *disguise* the opposite virtue in such a way as to make him like that, in preference to the sin he had so dearly loved. We are to *cheat* a sinner out of his sin, rather than compel him, under the stings of conviction, to give it up from deep-rooted principle" (168). Grimké responds further that the approach suggested by Beecher continues to victimize the victim and gives comfort to the sinner: "In other words, if one person is guilty of a sin against another person, I am to let the sinner go entirely unreproved, but to persuade the injured party to bear with humility and patience all the outrages that are inflicted upon him, and thus try to soothe the sinner into complacency with their goodness in bearing all things, and enduring all things" (168–69). It is this exchange, perhaps more than any other, that defines the dispute between Beecher and Grimké as it does between the Garrisonians and the gradualists. It also informs us about the characters in *Uncle Tom's Cabin*.

Some fifteen years after her sister Catharine had published her celebrated essay, Harriet Beecher Stowe continued to promote the gradualist argument in her novel *Uncle Tom's Cabin*. I began this essay by referring to the novel as an antislavery manifesto, and that it is. More than that, however, *Uncle Tom's Cabin* is a very effectively constructed piece of gradualist propaganda. Although clearly and passionately abolitionist, it displays even greater urgency in promoting gradualism and discrediting those who dared to call for immediate emancipation.

Tom and Eva as Ideals

Recall what Catharine Beecher had claimed to be the best way to change the hearts of the slaveholders. To Beecher, we should "render the . . . [slaves] so useful, so humble and unassuming, so kind in their feelings, and so full of love and good works, that prejudice would be supplanted by complacency in their goodness." (26–27). That, of course, sounds very much like Uncle Tom. As the story begins, we find that Tom's owner, Mr. Shelby, had reluctantly sold Tom and others to a slaver in order to save the plantation from creditors. The transaction would separate Tom from his fairly large and loving family. Bitterness and despair would have been the expected reaction to this news for most slaves, but Tom's reaction was different. Chloe asks, "What is you gwine do old man! What's to become of you?" Tom responds: "Him that saved Daniel in the den of lions—that saved the children in the fiery furnace—Him that walked on the sea and bade the winds be still—He's alive yet! and I've faith to believe He can deliver me. . . . The Lord is good unto all that trust Him, Chloe" (1.3). In this passage alone, Tom's reaction epitomizes the ideal slave in the Beecher model.

Eventually, Tom is sold again to a Mr. St. Clare. Here, Tom meets the other "ideal" figure in the drama, Little Eva, the young daughter of St. Clare. She is immediately taken with Tom's kindness and especially his Christian ways. Indeed, as their relationship grows they share a bond of faith. In explaining her bond with Tom, Eva reports to her father: "I've been up in Tom's room hearing him sing. . . . He sings such beautiful things, about the New Jerusalem, and bright angels, and the land of Canaan . . . and he's going to teach them to me. . . . He sings for me, and I read to him in my Bible, and he explains what it means" (2.2).

This relationship grows and Eva comes to expect spiritual guidance from Tom. Eva's health is not good, and as she grows worse, her spiritual ties to Tom become stronger. As she lies on her deathbed, she and Tom sing of the New Jerusalem, and Tom comforts her. At the moment before death Eva urgently whispers to her father: "Papa, these poor creatures love their children as much as you do me. Tom loves his children. Oh, do something for them. . . . And promise me, dear father, that Tom shall have his freedom as soon as—I am gone" (3.2). Tom's kindness and his good works have moved Eva on her deathbed to seek Tom's emancipation.

The development of these characters has followed precisely the course that Catharine Beecher would have prescribed. Tom is useful, humble, kind, and full of love and good works. Eva recognizes these qualities and does what she can to assure Tom's freedom. Tom is the ideal slave, and Eva represents the promise that gradualists argued would find a place in the hearts of slaveholders.

Things do not go well for Tom after Eva dies, however. He is not freed as Eva had hoped but is sold to the infamous Simon Legree. Legree's cruelty eventually leads to Tom's violent death. Even facing death, Tom still reflects the "ideal" attitude: "Don't call me poor fellow! I have been poor fellow; but that's all past and gone now. I'm right in the door going into glory! . . . Heaven has come! I've got the victory, the Lord has given it to me! (6.6). As he is dying, Tom displays the characteristics of the "elevated" slave. Catharine Beecher could not have imagined a more perfect example of a slave who would change the hearts of the slaveholder. Her sister Harriet provided in Tom's character the personification of the ideal Catharine only implied.

Topsy and Ophelia as Real-World Models

As compelling as their characters are, Tom and Eva remain almost too good to be true. Indeed they represent the ideal, almost mythic, figures that Stowe sets before her readers. They are Christ-like in their goodness. Stowe uses two other characters, however, to illustrate the potential of the gradualist approach to abolition. Stowe introduces Ophelia, Mr. St. Clare's sister (and interestingly a Northerner), to represent the prejudice against the slave. Ophelia knows little of slaves and avoids contact with them on her brother's plantation—that is, until St. Clare brings her Topsy, a young slave. Ophelia is overwhelmed. She exclaims: "Good gracious! what a heathenish, shiftless looking object! St. Clare, what in the world have you brought that thing here for? Your house is so full of these plagues now, that a body can't set down their foot without treading on 'em. I get up in the morning and find one asleep behind the door, and see one black head poking out from under the table. . . . What on earth did you want to bring this one for?" (2.2). Ophelia's response certainly does not reflect much sympathy for the unfortunate Topsy. Ophelia is a good example of the prejudiced slaveholder whom Beecher, through her model of action, hopes to change by elevating the character of the slave.

Topsy, on the other hand, epitomizes the "lowest" slave. She is uneducated and she possesses virtually no self-awareness other than her desire for immediate gratification. She steals and lies. At one point Topsy declares: "Never was born, tell you; never had no father, nor mother, nor nothin'. I war raised by a speculator, with lots of others. Old Aunt Sue used to take car on us" (2.2). So Topsy is a child who has had no direction, no love; she has no family and she has no understanding beyond the moment.

Topsy begins to see herself differently, however, as she interacts with Eva. Eva responds to Topsy with love and kindness, and Topsy, in turn, begins to steal less often and to resist lying. She even begins to realize her self-improvement. She tells Ophelia at one point that "I ain't half so wicked as I used to was" (4.2). As Topsy reforms, so does Ophelia. Ophelia becomes fond of Topsy, adopts her as her own child and takes her back to Vermont.

Topsy and Ophelia exemplify how "slave improvement" was to take place. Ophelia, the hardened bigot, and Topsy, the hopeless slave, are both elevated by Topsy's "improvement." Tom and Eva, by contrast, represent Stowe's abolition ideal—Tom the faithful slave and Eva the Christian, generous, understanding, and sympathetic mistress.

Conclusion

Harriet Beecher Stowe's *Uncle Tom's Cabin* represents a dramatic presentation of gradualist abolition rhetoric. It represented to a substantial mid-nineteenth-century audience the view that the best way to abolish slavery was through an effort to educate and improve the slaves. The work came at a time when the vitality of the abolitionist movement had waned considerably. It successfully reignited the movement. Its success came, however, at the expense of those within the movement who continued to insist that slaves bore no responsibility for their condition, that the slaveholders were the ones who should be educated and "improved." The gradualist tendency, which gained strength with the success of the novel and its dramatizations, dominated the movement thereafter.

Nevertheless, the success of Stowe's work brought renewed intensity to the slavery issue. One of the dramatizations of *Uncle Tom's Cabin* elicited the following review that appeared in the *New York Herald* on 3 September 1852: "The success of *Uncle Tom's Cabin* as a novel has naturally suggested its success upon the stage; but the fact has been overlooked, that any such representation must be an insult to the South—an exaggerated mockery of Southern institutions—and calculated, more than any other expedient of agitation, to poison the minds of our youth with the pestilent principles of abolitionism" (quoted in Moses and Brown 1934, 73). Clearly, *Uncle Tom's Cabin* created passion in both the North and the South. It sent an emotional arrow to the heart of slavery, and it dealt a deathblow to the militants within the antislavery movement who called for the immediate abolition of slavery.

Works Cited

Aiken, George L. [1852?] *Harriet Beecher Stowe's Uncle Tom's Cabin; or, Life among the Lowly: A Domestic Drama in Six Acts.* No other publication information available.

Beecher, Catharine. 1837. *An Essay on Slavery and Abolitionism.* Philadelphia: Henry Perkins.

Bormann, Ernest G. 1985. *The Force of Fantasy: Restoring the American Dream.* Carbondale: Southern Illinois University Press.

Grimké, Angelina. 1838. *Letters to Catharine E. Beecher: In Response to an Essay on Slavery and Abolitionism Addressed to A. E. Grimké.* Boston: Isaac Knapp.

Lewis, Gladys Sherman. 1994. *Message, Messenger and Response: Puritan Forms and Cultural Reformation in Harriet Beecher Stowe's* Uncle Tom's Cabin. New York: University Press of America.

Moses, Montrose, and John Mason Brown, eds. 1934. *The American Theatre as Seen by Its Critics, 1752–1934.* New York: W. W. Norton and Co.

Smith, Ralph R., and Russell R. Windes. 1993. "Symbolic Convergence and Abolitionism: A Terministic Reinterpretation." *Southern Speech Communication Association Journal* 59, no. 1:45–59.

———. 1995. "The Interpretation of Abolitionist Rhetoric: Historiography, Rhetorical Method and History." *Southern Speech Communication Association Journal* 60, no. 4:303–11.

Stowe, Lyman Beecher. 1934. *Saints, Sinners and Beechers.* Indianapolis: Bobs Merrill.

Walters, Ronald G. 1976. *The Anti-Slavery Appeal: American Abolitionism after 1830.* Baltimore: Johns Hopkins University.

Dario Fo's Angry Farce

Stanley Vincent Longman

ARCE, BY ITS very nature, is intensely social. It calls for direct address to the gathered public, surprising acrobatics, double takes, mimicry, speechifying, and other devices all thrown into the collective lap of the audience. No form seems emptier without an audience, and none can quite match the full resounding response a farce attains when it strikes home. Improvisational farce is even more intensely social, for it forms its twists and turns in direct response to the audience. Paradoxically, the best improvised farce is carefully prepared and rehearsed in anticipation of all variety of audience responses in order to make ready to incorporate them into performance. And some part of that preparation derives from the awareness that performers and audiences alike have of the world beyond the theatre.

This direct bond between performers and audience allows social issues to make their way easily onto the farcical stage. This, of course, does not always happen. Indeed, one tends to think of farce as empty, physical tomfoolery. In the hands of Dario Fo, however, improvised farce becomes an instrument of rhetorical dynamic with its audience. Characters are not psychological entities but rather forms that Fo may occupy through mimicry and then discard when convenient. They are types, with counterparts out there in the larger world: bosses, policemen, industrialists, workers, housewives, terrorists, anarchists, and scores of others. Dario Fo and his troupe play upon such recognition and carry their performances' implications beyond the confines of the particular theatre, or mere platform, into the society at large. This, in short, is drama at the service of rhetoric. Dario Fo has remarked that the popular theatre has always tended in this direction: " 'If you look into the original Greek theatre, you'll see that the popular stage has always used grotesqueries, satire, lampoons, and even—why not—scurrility to achieve its end of soiling, deflating, and bursting the balloon that the ruling class has always tried to keep pumped up.' Laughter, he likes to say, exposes the mind to 'the spikes of reason' " (quoted in Mann 1985, 105–6).

This essay explores Fo's approach to rhetorical farce. In his statement above, one might recognize a certain edge: his conception of farce draws on anger as a prime ingredient. The common phrase "outrageous farce" takes on a whole new meaning in Fo's work. It is not outrageous for forcing ordinary probability; it is outrageous for its basis in the spirit of outrage. Instead of outrageous farce, Fo's farce might be termed "outrage farce." In very general terms, it is farce that makes an ultimate appeal to reason through a spectacle of anarchy and suffering.

There is an apparent paradox in this kind of spectacle. After all, the worlds of Fo's plays consist of madmen and lunatics, persons going berserk. These characters are almost always set over against the upholders of "law and order." Ghigo De Chiara observed this paradox in a review of one of Fo's early works, his 1959 play *Gli arcangeli non giocano a flipper* (The Archangels Don't Play Pinball): "If it weren't for the liberal dose of madness he possesses, Fo would be a preacher, a moralist. Luckily for him (and us) he is a preaching clown. Farce represents a tool of moral corrosiveness for him, which, by its very nature, provides a pretext for escapism and paradoxical exercises. . . . But here all the congenial acrobatics of farce are rediscovered, along with some pointed references to reality" (1959, 39; all translations in this essay are the author's).

Fo himself has remarked, when confronted with this seeming paradox, that the inconsistency dissolves at once when you recognize that those in power would like to cancel reason and substitute for it a social order that is not to be disputed. The moment one forgets the role of laughter in society is the moment when reason dies of suffocation: "Irony is the requisite oxygen of reason" (Fo and Allegri 1990, 116–17). Fo insists that genuine satire is always based on an appeal to reason. He asserts that the society that is without tragedy is also without meaningful comedy. Both are based on a conviction of reason. Much of what passes for comic satire nowadays is superficial caricature that does nothing more than imitate the tics, walks, and mannerisms of the powerful, posing no more threat to them than perhaps taking them down a peg. Aristophanes and Molière, both of whom worked in societies noted for the grandeur of tragedy, wrote a kind of comedy rooted in reason. For them, comedy was an expression of outrage against hypocrisy, abuse of power, and humiliation. In their theatre, they never resorted to mere caricature, even in the case of a play like *The Clouds*. Fo has himself indulged in portraying real living people in his own blatant way, powerful personages such as Giovanni Agnelli in *Clacson, trombette e perlacchi* (Car Horns, Trumpets and Blown Raspberries) and Amintore Fanfani in *Il Fanfani rapito* (Fanfani Kidnapped), but not for the mere fun of imitation. Fo points out that one finds in Molière no cheap jokes based on aping the look or manner of powerful people but instead persistent and clear accusations of cheating and arrogant abuse of power in a social system that plays ruthlessly with death: "All of Molière's plays are pounded out in the tragic crucible with such ingredients as death, hunger, fear, superstition, myths and rituals" (Fo and Allegri 1990, 8–9).

Much of Fo's argument rests on this: that true comedy, real satire, attacks the most profound and disturbing forces that work on us. It is the obverse side of the coin of tragedy. Speaking of his play, *Morte accidentale di un anarchico* (Accidental Death of an Anarchist), Fo pointed out the close kinship of tragedy and satire, for both forms produce a type of catharsis different from that of ordinary drama: "The play was conceived in a grotesque style to avoid any dramatic catharsis. If we had created a dramatic play instead of a comic, grotesque and satirical play, we would have created another liberating catharsis. But this play doesn't allow you this outlet, because when you laugh, the sediment of anger stays inside you, and can't get out. Even the laughter won't liberate you. It's no wonder dictatorial governments always forbid laughter and satire first, rather than drama" (quoted in Meldolesi 1978, 179). One is reminded of the statement attributed to Bert Lahr when he looked up to see his audience doubled over in laughter: "Okay, laugh if you like, but this is funny!"

The concept is rhetorically very much akin to Bertold Brecht's *Verfremdungseffekt*, or the effect of making things strange. Here, the strangeness lies in the grotesque and farcical exaggeration, which may produce a cathartic release and yet never lets you forget that the source of the anger is still out there in the real world. Life itself is so riddled with perplexing mysteries that to confound it with corruption, hypocrisy, and abuse of power is unpardonable. At the same time, the basic necessities of life are so simple and so urgent that anyone lacking them cannot think beyond them. This is the humane base to Fo's farcical outrage.

This no doubt helps account for Fo's identification with the medieval *giullari*, the traveling minstrels of medieval Italy and with the *commedia dell'arte*. Fo was born in 1926 and grew up on the shores of Lake Maggiore near the Swiss border. The primary source of entertainment even then came from the story tellers, most of them fishermen of his home town or traveling performers. By his own account, these bawdy, raucous, irreverent tales—half told, half mimed—had a tremendous impact on him. They taught him, he has said, how to play with dialect and how to incorporate the real events of the moment into age-old stories on the spur of the moment (Fo and Allegri 1990, 20–24). Franca Rame, his wife and, virtually from the beginning of his career, his collaborator, was herself a *figlia d'arte,* the daughter of actors who had a tradition of improvised acting as traveling players. She has spoken of the influence the Rame family had on the development of methods in the Fo-Rame Company: "All the political arguments which Dario and I have developed had already been put into practice by my family a hundred years ago. They 'immersed' themselves in every town they toured. My grandfather, father and uncle Tommaso arrived in a city or a town, informed themselves about the history of the place, and then put it on stage" (1981, 61).

All of the plays that have come out of Fo and Rame's companies have exhibited these influences. Two in particular show a vivid indebtedness. One is *Comica finale* (Comic Finale), a very early play. This production came about when Gianfranco de Bosio of the Teatro Stabile of Turin invited Fo to present a series of improvised comic sketches. Fo had access to the *canovacci* (scenarios) of the Rame family. He chose four of them, did research on the appropriate manner of presentation, and presented them with tremendous success in December of 1958. The other example is his famous *Mistero buffo* (Funny Mystery Play), one of Fo's masterpieces, first performed in 1969 and still in his repertory. Fo performs these several tales all alone both as narrator and multiple impersonator (with the one exception of the story of Mary at the Cross in angry discussion with the Archangel Gabriel about all the trouble he has caused her; this is performed by Franca Rame). The piece derives from the tales of the medieval *giullari,* tales that were often anticlerical versions of the biblical stories, retold from the perspective of the little people who might have witnessed the passion of Christ. In the course of his telling the story of the raising of Lazarus, for example, he becomes a visitor to the cemetery where Lazarus was buried, an incensed grounds keeper, members of Lazarus's family who lie to Jesus about how long Lazarus has been dead, and even the stinking, maggoty Lazarus himself. In the same play, Fo assumes the role of a Ruzante-like *zanni,* crazy with hunger, who mimes eating his own eyeball, his hand, his foot, his intestines, his audience, the mountains, even God Himself, then imagines himself preparing an enormous feast in great caldrons, only to end up having to eat a tiny housefly.

There is another dimension to farce that Fo taps with no small delight. That is its spirit of camaraderie. It creates a chaotic, joyously shared revelry. It produces a feeling of "us versus them." Farce is a natural form of the rhetoric of the powerless: it creates a mayhem that shatters the imposed social order, and it exposes the irrationality of the powerful. Unable literally to tear apart the fabric of society, we are allowed to do so figuratively through farce. And so the platform stage of farce becomes an arena for the torture of bureaucrats, politicians, clergy, policemen, military brass, industrialists and any other purveyors of the established order responsible for the sorry state the world is in. These, of course, are the descendants of Pantalone, the Capitano, and the Dottore.

The evolution of the Fo-Rame career illustrates a drive to enhance this spirit of camaraderie in every way possible. In very general terms one may divide this development into four phases. The first, from 1953 to 1963, consisted of revue sketches and short satirical farces such as *I cadaveri si spediscono, le donne si spogliono* (Cadavers Are to Be Shipped Off, Women Undressed, 1959), about illegal divorce agencies infiltrated by transvestite detectives, or *Gli arcangeli non giocano a flipper* (Archangels Don't Play Pinball, 1960), a madcap portrait of the Milanese underworld populated by whores, pimps, schemers and white-collar bureaucrats. This period capped out with Fo and Rame joining the popular television variety show, *Conzonissima,* produced by the national television network, Radio Italiana (RAI). The enormous success they had during their brief stay with the show gave them a large national following. One skit they performed for the show dealt with "occupational hazards" of industry and depicted a lady's fall into the machinery of a meat packing plant. The machinery couldn't be stopped so she emerged nicely ground and packed in cans, which her nephew was allowed to take home as a remembrance. The piece provoked the ire of the meat processors and they prevailed on RAI to exercise control over Fo and Rame. The resultant censorship led Fo and Rame to walk out after less than two months on the show (Valentini 1977, 77–84).

The second phase began then as the Fo-Rame company took to the stage with *Isabella, tre caravelle e un cacciaballe* (Isabella, Three Ships and a Con-man), an ambitious, epic-style play exposing the narrow interests and absurd schemes that sent Christopher Columbus off on his expedition to the Indies. During the 1963–64 season the play toured the major theatres of Italy (except those in Genoa, Columbus's home town, where the play was banned). It was followed by a number of other elaborate productions, such as *La colpa è sempre del diavolo* (It's Always the Devil's Fault, 1965) and *La Signora è da buttare* ("The Lady's to Be Thrown Out," 1967). These all had splendid, imaginative sets and costumes designed by Fo, who also directed and starred. They played in the prestigious grand old box-pit-and-gallery theatres of the Italian circuit to titillated middle-class and well-to-do audiences.

The great upheavals of 1968 brought on the third phase. Fo and Rame abandoned the circuit and began to play to working-class audiences in found spaces: on farms, in factories, in city squares, in mess halls, and in parks on the occasions of the Communist Party's Festivals of *Unità*. Fo declared at the time his reason for the change: "We were fed up with being court jesters for the *bourgeoisie,* for whom our critique of society had become mere Alka Seltzer. So we decided to become instead the court jesters of the proletariat" (quoted in Valentini 1977, 8). The Fo-Rame Company was renamed *Nuova Scena,* and it operated on generous subsidies from the cultural arm (ARCI) of the Communist Party. Out of this relationship came a number of didactic "learning pieces," such as *L'operaio conosce trecento parole il padrone mille per questo lui è padrone* (The Worker Knows Three Hundred Words, the Boss a Thousand, and That's Why He's Boss," 1969), a lesson on the need for education, or *Tutti uniti! Tutti insieme! Ma scusa, quello non è il padrone?* (Everyone United! Everyone Together! Hold On, Isn't That Fellow the Boss? 1971), a lesson on the working class movement between 1911 and the advent of fascism in 1922. In these and other plays, Fo managed to arouse the ire of the Communist Party leadership, which recognized its own people ridiculed as self-serving, smug bureaucrats, slow to rally behind the students, the women's movement, or the call for environmental protection. The Party first denounced *Nuova Scena,* then withdrew support. The company took on a new name, *Il Collettivo la Comune,* and continued without subsidy. The plays continued to be highly topical critiques of Italian society, or even world politics, including the treatment of the Palestinians or the revolution and subsequent oppression in Chile. Mixed in among them were a number of plays developed out of the spirit of the *giullari* and the *commedia dell'arte,* most of them one-man shows like *Mistero buffo* (Funny Mystery Play, 1969) or *Fabulazzo osceno* (Obscene Fable, 1981).

Beginning in the late 1970s and continuing today are a series of plays that focus on the domestic scene and use allusions to the outside society to develop the continuing critique of society. The first play in this mode was *Non si paga! Non si paga!* (Can't Pay! Won't Pay!, 1974, revised in 1980), and there have been several since, some written with Franca Rame, such as *Tutto casa letto e chiesa* (It's All Home, Bed and Church, 1977, revised 1981), and some by Franca Rame alone, such as *Parliamo di donne* (Let's Talk about Women, 1977). Some of Fo's more recent plays deal with women of power: *Quasi per caso una donna,*

Elisabetta (Elizabeth, Almost by Chance a Woman, 1984), *Il ratto della Francesca* (The Abduction of Francesca, 1986), or *Il Papa e la strega* (The Pope and the Witch, 1989). Still more recently Fo has been collaborating with Franca Rame and their son Jacopo on monologue plays such as *Sex? Don't Mind if I Do.* Ironically, in the midst of these pieces dealing with feminist liberation, the marriage of Fo and Rame seemed to fall apart with her announcement on national television in 1987 of her intent to divorce. At any rate there has been no divorce.

These phases are not rigid. In terms of technique and style, the work of Fo and Rame has maintained a strong continuity. There are plays of five different types, all of them appearing scattered through the span of over forty years that these two have dominated the Italian stage. They include revue sketches (such as *L'operaio conosce trecento parole . . .*), fables (such as *Mistero buffo*), theatre of fact, based on actual events or at least actual people (such as *Clacson, trombette, pernacchi,* dealing with a hypothetical kidnapping of Fiat boss, Giovanni Agnelli), historical "revisionist" drama (such as *Isabella* or *Elisabetta*), and finally domestic plays (such as *Non si paga!* or *Coppia aperta*). Cut another way, the plays may be seen as either topical satires or more general protests against the age-old abuse of power, presented as fables or histories.

What binds the productions together is the special approach that the Fo-Rame company (whatever name it may go under) has taken to improvised satirical farce. The creative method of the company has not changed significantly over the years. To be sure, there is a considerable surface difference between the spectacular theatricalism of *Isabella, tre caravelle e un cacciaballe* and the rough simplicity of *Mistero buffo,* but there is an underlying rhetorical function to this improvised comedy. The special techniques and devices adopted to create these spectacles serve to reenforce an act of persuasion. The plays have a rough-and-tumble quality. They make no attempt at a sustained illusion and constantly remind the audience that they are witnessing a performance. Dario Fo may amble out onto the stage before the show starts. The spotlights are still out, the stage still bare, and no show seems planned. He engages the audience with his own banter. Sometimes he will single out a particular audience member and deal directly with that person so as to have a sort of ally on through the show. Meanwhile other actors begin to arrive here and there. They begin to take out banners, properties, musical instruments, bits of costuming, and as they complete this work, the lights come up and Fo joins them. Even after the show is underway, Fo will break from the action to make comments to the audience. This device, made famous by Ettore Petrolini as the *slittamento,* consists of breaking abruptly from the action to talk about the show itself, one of the other actors, a member of the audience, or some current event and then, just as abruptly, returning to the world of the play. Of course, many of these *slittamenti* are well rehearsed even if invented that very day in order to incorporate a late-breaking news item.

Closely allied with this technique is Fo's use of sudden transformations. He will at one moment be engaged in conversation with an imaginary second person and, in a shot, will become that other person. He may pantomime the presence of unseen objects, even several at one time. These, too, engage the audience through play on the collective imagination.

One other device for which Fo is well known is his so-called *grammelot*. The term is Italian theatrical jargon for a form of speech consisting of nonsense syllables, spoken with such inflection, onomatopoeia, and sheer expressiveness that the audience cannot help but understand. The idea is not original with Fo, but he employs it in his own rich, inimitable manner. As Roberto Nipoti puts it, the *grammelot* turns the usual functions of words and gestures upside down: instead of the words clarifying gesture, gestures become a type of subtitle for the words (Nepoti 1982, 9).

Fo is fond of calling his plays *pezzi da bruciare,* literally pieces to be burnt up, or, as Suzanne Cowan puts it, "throw-away theatre" (Cowan 1975, 102). They are pieces laced with allusions to specific events in the outside world, and they are either discarded or updated with new references as the need arises. If the play is to be produced elsewhere—Berlin, Paris, London, New York—it has to be reshaped to suit that new context. Fo was pleased with the London adaptation of *Accidental Death of an Anarchist* because it incorporated such new allusions, and he was displeased with the New York version, which dispensed with almost all allusions (Fo and Allegri 1990, 150). Enlisting the audience in the spectacle, then referring them to the political and social world beyond, gives the theatrical event great resonance.

Fo speaks of criticism that he received from fellow Marxists for putting on *Mistero buffo* on the grounds that the religious stories and allusions are out of place in any theatre meaningful in present-day society. Religion, after all, is the opiate of the proletariat. Fo retorted that it is they who have gone off the road: "I recall that it was a certain Antonio Gramsci who insisted that if you don't know where you've been, you'll have trouble understanding where you want to go. This matter of the magical relationship with nature, with the earth, with myth, with religiosity, is part and parcel of the history of the working class. You can't just cross it out. It's our duty to study it, to recapture it to make it sensible and actual in terms of its important values" (Fo and Allegri

1990, 140–41). And indeed, he felt vindicated by the enthusiastic response he received with the play. This heightened sensitivity to audiences enables Fo to meet them on their own terms and carry forward his rhetorical buffoonery.

It is probably no accident that the upheavals of 1968 produced a rebirth in Italy of improvised farce. By that year Dario Fo and Franca Rame had long ago established that form as their own. For the Italian theatre generally, however, the spirit of improvised farce had been nearly suffocated during the years of fascism and even in the postwar years of reconstruction. The upheavals of 1968, with the student uprisings, factory takeovers, terrorist acts of the Red Brigade, and renewed fascist activity, produced such outrage, terror, and uncertainty that Italy was never to be the same again. Every aspect of society was affected, the theatre included. Perhaps the most productive way for theatre to respond to such social unrest is by relieving the audience's sense of helplessness and frustration through improvised farcical spectacles, shows that address social issues and resolve them with hilarity. They were shows, too, that grew out of the populace, as if there were a primary need to get back to folk roots. The working people, who had been so much a part of the medieval street shows of the *giullari* first, then of Angelo Beolco and the later *commedia dell'arte*, can remind us once again of the common sense and earthy values that society and its institutions had abandoned and even squelched. Improvised farce has the supreme advantage of allowing both the fictive spectacle of working-class victory and the open exchange of energies with a real working-class audience. The techniques and material that Dario Fo developed for his particular variety of improvised farce served as a model and a challenge for others. Even those who developed different techniques did so with awareness of Fo's work. Some have turned to a more rigorous commedia style—artists such as Alessandro Marchetti and Luisella Sala of Milan, or the Teatro alla Giustizia of Mestre outside Venice, or the Piccionaia of the Carrara family in Vicenza. Others have taken the improvisational techniques and applied them to revision of classical plays, giving them a new relevance. Foremost among these are the Teatro Due in Parma and Puppi e Fresedde of Angelo Savelli in Florence. Finally, there are those who have adopted techniques close to Fo's, such as Paolo Rossi or the members of the Teatro dell'Elfo in Milan.

These are tributes to the pioneering Fo has accomplished in rediscovering the power of farce once it is infused with an appropriate mix of anger and hilarity. Fo's are intensely social plays, both in the act of peformance and in the implications they carry about the larger society beyond the bounds of the immediate place of performance. Despite their madness, their sheer lunacy, they are ultimately civilized and supremely rational. He reminds us that the human capacity for laughter serves to undermine such excesses as bloated power, self-serving hypocrisy, and mean-spirited cruelty. Laughter restores our rational equilibrium.

Works Cited

Cowan, Suzanne. 1975. "The Throw-Away Theatre of Dario Fo." *Drama Review* 19, no. 2 (June): 102–13.

De Chiara, Ghigo. 1959. Review of *Gli arcangeli non giocano a flipper. Sipario,* September.

Fo, Dario, and Luigi Allegri. 1990. *Dialogo provocatorio sul comico, il tragico, la follia e la ragione.* Rome and Bari: Editore Giuseppe Laterza e Figli.

Mann, Charles C. 1985. "The Red Mime of Milan." *Atlantic,* September, 3.

Meldolesi, Claudio. 1978. *Su un comico in rivolta Dario Fo il bufalo il bambino.* Rome: Bulzoni Editore.

Nepoti, Roberto. 1982. "Ridi con rabbia." In *Dario Fo,* ed. Marina Cappa and Roberto Nepoti, 7–17. Rome: Gremese Editore.

Rame, Franca. 1981. Essay in *Domenica del Corriere,* September 26.

Valentini, Chiara. 1977. *La storia di Dario Fo.* Milan: Feltrinelli.

Stain upon the Silence

Samuel Beckett's Deconstructive Inventions

Leigh Anne Howard

*I*N THE LAST twenty years numerous studies about deconstruction theory have torn apart texts and hierarchies in order to gain insights about texts, contexts, and society. Some scholars have valued deconstruction theory as a key critical method for analyzing public address, organizational cultures, literary discourse, and dramatic productions. This method questions surface or superficial messages and encourages the reader to explore signals hidden below the surface. For example, theatre scholars who follow this branch of deconstruction place faith in the audience's experience and ability to make sense of what they see and hear; they remove authority from the playwright and relocate it with the audience. Other scholars regard deconstruction as a philosophy of language, a perspective that attempts to dislocate linear patterns of communicating; that explores binary oppositions; that questions the play of words, language, and meaning. This branch of scholars, for instance, seeks to fracture the chain of linear messages in a way that undermines plot, sequence, and action that we traditionally value in Western theatre.

Following in the tradition of Jacques Derrida and his play on *différance* (see Derrida 1978), I propose another perspective that positions deconstruction as both a method and a philosophy but not in the ways I have just outlined. This alternative viewpoint transforms deconstruc-

The author would like to thank Judith D. Hoover, Pat Carr, and Larry Winn for their comments about earlier drafts of this article and for an enthusiasm that resulted in its publication.

tion, from a methodological approach used to explain or critique discourse, into basic philosophical assumptions and strategies authors use as they compose their communication. Deconstruction becomes a method of and a philosophy about invention.

Using the early plays of Samuel Beckett, I explore deconstructive invention, or the use of deconstruction to create messages. First, I summarize deconstruction because I suggest that deconstructive inventors use processes previously associated with deconstructive criticism to reveal their own beliefs and to shape the beliefs of their audience. Second, I position Samuel Beckett as an exemplar of deconstructive invention by exploring images and ideas in his early plays. Furthermore, I explain that Beckett uses rhetorical or literary tropes—metonymy, synecdoche, metaphor, and irony—for audience members to interpret the difference between literal language and action and the figurative messages and experience they encounter. Finally, I suggest that deconstructive invention prompts the audience into taking action upon what they see. Understanding is no longer paramount, but action, building, reconstructing—a step beyond understanding—is the goal.

Defining Deconstruction

Formal studies of deconstruction start with Jacques Derrida, who uses deconstruction to critique western culture's adherence to social structures and convention. In particular, he criticizes promoting specific ideas of meaning, denying history, and separating subject (and subsequent awareness) from object (see Bannet 1989, 184–227). Derrida works to collapse hierarchy and oppositional pairings, and he believes that the relationship between sign and signifier is precarious, unstable, and multivocal (Bannet 1989, 184); therefore, the relationship between words and reality constantly changes. Thus, meanings are not self-contained entities because meanings are closely intertwined with a language that endlessly traces to other meanings and words, depending on specific contextual elements. As a result, Derrida, following Heidegger, is critical of philosophical humanism that creates privilege, hierarchy, autonomy, or universal essence.

Deconstructionist criticism defines a text as a pattern established by previous readings, a pattern that readers must uncover because its rules and grammar are obscured. In that spirit a text—created by an author who has definite, personal involvement with the text—must be "reconstructed" by audiences. Furthermore, this reconstruction obviously differs from the author's construction; hence, audiences become active participants in the work. Jonathan Culler explains that deconstructionists place meaning not within the text, but within audience members, who must base interpretation of the entire production on their individual experiences. In addition, the deconstructive critic declines the authority position; therefore, one "truth" or meaning does not exist (see Culler 1982; Scholes 1988; Schusterman 1988).

By destroying hierarchy—one truthful interpretation—deconstruction criticism establishes a lack of faith in logic because logic may not provide meaning to every audience member and because logic may not prompt the audience to act upon what they see. As a result connections between actions, language, and the reader's or viewer's consciousness assume prime importance, but the sequence of action and language do not (Culler 1982, 110, 181, pass.). Instead of following a syllogistic pattern leading to a logical conclusion, deconstructionists suggest that rearranging actions and words does not affect meaning. Because the text itself is not all-important and because words or utterances themselves do not make meaning, their arrangement becomes superfluous because neither words nor structure instill or prevent meaning. Moreover, a jumbled arrangement may provoke readers to reconstruct what they see rather than settling for understanding. Reconstruction is more active than passive understanding.

Deconstruction's impact on theatre involves questioning nearly every aspect of traditional Western theatre (Constantinidis 1993, 83). As Stratos Constantinidis writes, traditional theatre privileges origin and gives the playwright specific rights regarding the use and/or interpretation of theatre texts (14). The playtext is considered a complete entity that actors use to interpret a playwright's vision. With deconstruction, the importance of the playwright or playtext becomes negligible. Deconstruction seeks to disrupt the flow that situates the playwright as creator of the text that directors/designers envision for the actors, who then interpret the vision for audience members. Chaos, circularity, and ambiguity, for example, are the marks of a theatre under deconstruction. Or, such a theatre may involve breaking the language barrier (Pountney 1988, 5) in ways that focus on subtexts, action, and symbols. In any case, to understand a dramatic work and to take action after experiencing a performance, audience members complete the work, examine what happens onstage, and transcend the work to understand how the work affects them. Audience members learn to "read" (de Man 1982, 10) the text (images and actions), submerse themselves in the experience, and let their imaginations create the message.

Instead of analyzing a work by reversing convention, denying authority, and enhancing individual experience, a deconstructive author *creates* the work with these techniques. By utilizing such unconventional methods, deconstructive authors provide thought-provoking material for audiences to interpret and to correlate to their own experiences, and to establish meaning for. For instance, a playwright may show a character's mental dexterity by choosing to develop physically immobile characters; to understand and make meaning the audience members must attend the character's dialogue and mental capabilities. Thus, like a deconstructive critic, a deconstructive author undermines the obvious focal point or message in order to explore covert messages that remain obscured.

Furthermore, deconstructive authors resist becoming authorities about their own works. They refuse to explain the meaning of their works and suggest that no true answer to the dramatic riddle exists. This type of author self-deprecates in order to defend the reader's or audience's position, to overthrow an overbearing, authoritarian tyrant (i.e., traditional rules), or to condemn publicly literary convention. Like other postmodern literature, deconstructive inventions, regardless of whether the audience knows or recognizes the fact, reflect an author's experience and worldview. Thus, deconstructive invention poses another genre of literature and implies new ways to convey meaning and ideas.

Beckett and Deconstructive Invention

Usually critics link Samuel Beckett with modern, existential, and absurdist schools of thought. Indeed, solitude, failure, chaos, tension, and the deteriorating human condition, as well as agony, disharmony, and death form themes that pervade Beckett's work (see Webb 1982; Dearlove 1985; McCarthy 1985). The paradoxical nature of his works, however, reveals the applicability of deconstruction techniques. Although a few scholars have addressed Beckett in postmodern terms (Axelrod 1992; Begam 1992; Rabinovitz 1992; Zurbrugg 1990; Connor 1988), few have explored deconstruction as it relates either to Beckett's dramatic works or to composition in general. Also, as Beckett's work increasingly strips away dramatic elements, his later plays might be more easily aligned with postmodernism. Examination of Beckett's early plays, however—including *Waiting for Godot* (1953), *Endgame* (1957), *Krapp's Last Tape* (1958), *Happy Days* (1961), *Play* (1963), and *Not I* (1972)—suggests that Beckett's role as a deconstructive playwright began early in his career. Although his works predate formal studies of deconstruction by nearly thirty years, Beckett's devices parallel the subversion, play, and dislocation characteristic of deconstruction.

Although not carrying the analysis through in terms of deconstructive tenets, Gontarski (1983) does identify how Beckett enjoys breaking the notion of binary oppositions. For example, Gontarski cites Beckett's rejection of mimesis along with his unwillingness to abandon representation completely (5). Gontarski also explains that autobiography and self-disclosure repelled Beckett, yet Beckett scholars have long speculated on the personal evident in his drama. Finally, Gontarski discusses Beckett's rejection of artificiality and previous literary forms, which contrasts with his elaborate network of pattern and allusion. I extend this observation: Beckett experiments with *différance*. He playfully explores the area between realism and surrealism in his dramatic works. They are not realistic, yet they cannot be discarded as irrelevant to our lived experience. Beckett wavers between the private and public, realizing that public life (playwriting) depends on the private for inspiration, even though he hopes to retain his privacy from the public. Finally, he rejects literary convention and seeks alternative conventions to adopt. For Beckett, plays do not represent abstract ideas; they abstractly describe ways in which people experience and live (Webb 1972, 1). Beckett also grapples with contradictions and authority. Known as a playwright who guards his texts against directors and aesthetic distortion, he has frequently rejected an authoritarian role by not imposing his intentions upon audiences. For instance, when American director (and Beckett's close personal friend) Alan Schneider questioned the identity of "Godot" in *Waiting for Godot,* Beckett replied that had he known he would have put it in the play (Schneider 1958). In fact, as Martin Esslin wrote, "No writer of our times has more consistently refused to comment on, or explain, his own work than Beckett" (1965, 1). Hence, as deconstruction theory suggests, Beckett empowers his audience and validates diverse, individual interpretation.

Searching for Expression

Early in his career Beckett explained his distrust of language. Like the deconstructionists who followed, Beckett said that words restricted his own expression: "There is nothing to express, nothing with which to express, no power to express, no desire to express, together with the obligation to express" (Beckett and Duthuit 1965, 17). Many modern and existential critics interpret this quotation to mean that Beckett struggled to escape the meaninglessness that surrounds words; however, this statement could also refer to the overwhelming power of language. Language wrestles the ability to shape ideas and action from the hands of the author. Words assume a voice of their own; they do not always precisely reflect the author's intention and voice. Thus, if words were so slippery, Beckett needed another mode of communication to help audiences understand and act upon his literature.

This need for precise communication could have been the impetus behind Beckett's move from fiction to drama. Perhaps Beckett abandoned fiction with its sole reliance on language to communicate, and adopted drama, that also incorporated sound and sight, to escape his distrust and to retain more artistic control over audience experience. After years of questioning and struggling to express, Beckett said, "I glimpsed the world that I had to create in order to be able to breathe" (quoted in Juliet 1989–90, 18). With drama, therefore, Beckett obtained tools in addition to words to shape messages more accurately and to capture audience attention.

By relying on drama's shape and form rather than information and language, Beckett encouraged audiences to experience the work. "I am interested in the shape of ideas even if I do not believe them," he said. "It is the shape that matters" (quoted in Hobson 1956, 153). Beckett requires audiences to suspend logic and reason. They must refrain from unraveling the play's details and absorb the total dramatic experience. Only by becoming totally absorbed can audiences really experience the work. Once people know the information (or how the story ends), they are less ready to experience and repeat the work. Conversely, when audiences do not completely understand a work, they may eagerly continue to explore the work until they find connections between stage and real life.

Relying on Rhetorical Tropes

Despite their wordless and actionless characteristics, Beckett's plays do contain guideposts that assist audiences in making connections. He uses rhetorical tropes or devices, such as metonymy, synecdoche, metaphor, and irony, as tools for deconstructive invention with which he forms a visual framework. The audience may use this framework to uncover the differences between the literal language and action and the figurative messages and experience. Michael Osborn writes that these devices serve "to animate whatever rhetorical reasonings" developed out of specific thought structures and goals (1976, 3). While Osborn explains the success of the tropes because of their "perspective by congruity," these tropes also become successful in Beckett's works by revealing incongruities that converge to create the total performance. As rhetorical tropes highlight incongruities, they allow Beckett, as well as audience members, the freedom to invent what Tom Bishop calls the "poetic depiction of our fate" (1969, 27).

Metonymy

Metonymy appears when authors substitute concrete words, images, and ideas for abstract words, images, and ideas. Beckett produces concrete onstage actions to describe the abstract concept of life and existence. Vladimir and Estragon represent all humans who remain unaware of their situations; Hamm and Clov represent humans who refuse to take action. Krapp symbolizes those who deny, and Winnie symbolizes those who ignore. Through metonymy, authors can represent people and actions offstage through characters and actions onstage. As characters refuse to recognize and to resolve their dire circumstances, they face a bleak future. They face a dilemma between recognition and denial, and they can escape neither. Again, they waver in their decision-making process; they remain in a fuzzy area of *différance* that is neither here nor there.

Synecdoche

The most obvious examples of synecdoche in Beckett involve the use of a mouth in *Not I* to represent Mouth's intrapersonal voice, heads in *Play* to represent entire characters, and "Brownie" the revolver in *Happy Days* to represent death and destruction. Synecdoche can also be seen in *Krapp's Last Tape*, where Beckett reduces forty-odd years of memory to several audio tape reels. In addition, Beckett restricts dramatic action to a small part of the stage instead of utilizing the full stage area. Although critics consider synecdoche a traditional rhetorical device, Beckett experiments with this trope in untraditional ways. He creates incongruous images that seize audiences and leave them unsatisfied and confused. This confusion prompts audience members to continue to explore the work.

Metaphor

Osborn describes metaphor as a tool that "causes the mind to pause in its normally efficient processing of sense-data [and] to visualize the symbolic aberration presented to it" (Osborn 1976, 6). He adds that metaphor organizes and influences perception as well as disturbs the patterns constituting what humans accept as reality. Moreover, Osborn identifies light and dark images as powerful archetypal meta-phors, characterized by universal appeal, embodiment of human moti-vation, unchanging pattern, and prominence in features of human ex-perience.

Beckett capitalizes on the light/dark family of archetypal metaphors to shape an unstable world in need of change and reform. For instance, in *Waiting for Godot*, Beckett uses darkness to echo the ignorance of his characters. Vladimir and Estragon, lacking the mentality to recog-nize the problems they face, live in a dark world. Beckett's characters think more as his plays progress, and Beckett increases his stage light-ing to emphasize this progression. After *Happy Days*, however, Beckett's characters continue to think, but that thought becomes insular or self-centered. The characters do not consider the problems facing all humans (i.e., a deteriorating world and superficial existence); instead, they reflect on their own grievances and circumstances, which have no connec-tion to others. Beckett uses a spotlight to underscore the isolated, self-centered thought. As a character speaks the spotlight focuses only on that character. Otherwise, the characters live in gloomy, bleak darkness with no chance to escape. Thus, all of his characters lack an ability to speak in an encompassing, socially meaningful, or thoughtful way; yet, they lack the ability to remain silent. They fluctuate in that fuzzy area, unable to speak and unable to be quiet.

Irony

Of all rhetorical tropes, irony seems most appropriate for deconstruc-tive inventors, and for Beckett in particular, as they construct incon-gruous images. Because irony assumes the role of "all-purpose, slot filler," this rhetorical trope becomes useful whenever people want to be vague, indirect, or unassertive (Booth 1983, 721). Kenneth Burke also sees irony as a way to rationalize an author's simultaneous feelings of humility and superiority. He explains that the author's humility (his or her recognition that people would not exist without ideas) counterbal-ances the author's feelings of superiority for creating the work. Fur-thermore, Burke adds, the author neglecting irony becomes sacrificed to the literal (Burke 1969).

Acknowledging that irony may or may not be intentional, Wayne Booth illustrates irony's role in literature when he describes two genres of irony: stable irony and unstable irony. According to Booth, stable irony depends on the audience's sharing norms with the author and other readers, requires a definite message that the audience must recon-struct, and does not encourage the audience to elaborate on that reconstruction; unstable irony suggests that readers cannot share interpretation by reconstructing messages. Instead, audience members must build individually on the information presented and construct their own individual meanings (Booth 1974, 240 and pass.). Beckett uses unstable irony to avoid a single, truthful meaning and reason. Beckett encourages infinite elaboration of his works in order for audiences to uncover numerous interpretations. For example, audience members may choose to speculate about Hamm's and Clov's interest in the world outside of their shelter. The characters seem fascinated with the actions they see through the window, but they elect to remain indoors. In this instance audience members can satisfy their own curiosity through their own speculation even though characters refrain from doing so.

Seeking Audience Expression

To be an artist, Beckett writes, is to fail, since the artist strives to leave the logical world, "the domain of the feasible," and to embrace the imagination (quoted in Ben-Zvi 1986, 32). Beckett calls on audience members to embrace his imagination, then to abandon his imagination by creating their own vision. He encourages audience members to outguess him in interpreting the dramatic riddle he places before them. Audience members must bring their own experiences to the theatre, and they must relate to the stage action or nonaction before transcending those connections to create an entirely new experience.

This type of interaction forms an integral part of deconstructive invention. Deconstructive inventors such as Beckett call on what Gaston Bachelard calls the "poetic imagination" (1969, xi–xxxiii). Poetic imagination, in contrast to reason and science, looks toward the future by describing the "threshold of being" and "reverberation of experience" (Bachelard 1969, xii). With such audience action, performance assumes a new role with endless possibilities. No longer is drama a mimetic tool that represents life, nor is it a type of *poiesis* that encourages audience members and performers to understand or to construct culture and personal identity. Instead, drama becomes a type of *kinesis*, a tool for revolution and change (Conquergood 1992, 84). Performance as *kinesis* implies an urgent motivation for performance to break, then remake, social structures that perpetuate oppression. Beckett's plays provide this type of motivation for action. For example, characters in all of Beckett's early plays can be seen as synecdochic expressions of audiences who do not act. Like the characters, if audiences do not act, they may become insular, self-centered, consumed by a world that feels no compunction for bypassing them. Thus, as a tool for social intervention, performance is a way to exact change in addition to suggesting change. This type of performance is "no longer stable and structured, because it fluctuates, changes, and improvises to meet the needs of people in specific situations and societies" (Howard 1995, 10).

This shift toward *kinesis*, with its focus on action and intervention, has several correlations to deconstruction. First, power is decentered; intention of players and director is subverted, and what the audience makes of the performance becomes the primary focus. Second, audience members must engage in deconstruction. They must break down the actions they see, connect those actions onstage to their own experiences, then reconstruct the performance to generate their own meaning and to initiate change. Only after mentally breaking and remaking performed action can *they* take "real world" action. Third, the director or playwright who wishes to spur audiences to action must be able to compose performance problems precisely. That is, they, too, must go through the breaking and remaking phases as they construct. One tool they may use entails rhetorical tropes. Deconstruction supports the notion that rhetorical tropes and figurative language do not exist as mere decoration. The tropes, instead, help deconstructive inventors shape and define audience experience. They comprise definite tools a rhetor may use to tap into audience members' emotions and to extract a response or action, whether the action consists of awareness, investigation, or active reform. Each of these correlations points to deconstruction as a philosophy as it forms a basis for action in addition to the mode of action. Audiences approach theatre with the assumption that they must embrace the theatrical experience. They acknowledge the necessity of breaking, constructing, and reconstructing; indeed, these three components of *kinesis* are mandatory components of the theatre experience. Audience members know that in a world that constantly changes, they, too, must not only meet the change but take charge of the change. They work toward self-assertion by engaging in a process that requires them to examine what they see, divide those images into discreet units, sort the helpful from the archaic, then assemble a new vision for the world they inhabit. Deconstruction, then, provides a base for how audiences approach theatre, how they consume the drama, and how they react to the experience. Deconstruction provides a framework for the actions they see as well as any actions they take.

Deconstructive inventors such as Samuel Beckett construct a new stage for audience members to explore. They help audiences rediscover a world they thought they knew. These writers indicate that "against and in spite of the harshness and uncertainty," human will, spirit, and humor provide a "glimmer of hope" in the dark abyss in which humans find themselves (Schneider 1958, 19). These writers feel compelled to describe the world they see. As Beckett remarked, "I couldn't have done it otherwise. Gone on, I mean. I could not have gone through the awful wretched mess of life without having left a stain upon the silence" (quoted in Bair 1990, 640).

Works Cited

Axelrod, M. R. 1992. *The Politics of Style in the Fiction of Balzac, Beckett, and Cortazar*. New York: St. Martin's Press.

Bachelard, Gaston. 1969. *The Poetics of Space*. Trans. Maria Jolas. Boston: Beacon Press.

Bair, Deirdre. 1990. *Samuel Beckett*. New York: Simon and Schuster.

Bannet, Eve Tavor. 1989. *Structuralism and the Logic of Dissent*. Chicago: University of Chicago Press.

Beckett, Samuel. [1953] 1976. *Waiting for Godot*. Repr. in *I Can't Go On, I'll Go On*, ed. Richard Seaver, 365–476. New York: Grove Press.

———. [1957] 1981. *Endgame*. Repr. in *Stages of Drama*, ed. Carl Klaus, Miriam Gilbert, and Bradford S. Fields, Jr., 926–51. Glenview, IL: Scott Foreman and Company.

———. [1958] 1960. *Krapp's Last Tape*. Repr. in *Krapp's Last Tape and Other Dramatic Pieces*, 9–28. New York: Grove Press.

———. [1961] 1988. *Happy Days*. Repr. in *The Drama: Traditional and Modern*, ed. Mark Goldman and Isadore Traschen, 661–86. Boston: Allyn and Bacon, Inc.

———. [1963] 1970. *Play*. Repr. in *Cascando and Other Short Dramatic Pieces*, 45–63. New York: Grove Press.

———. [1972] 1976. *Not I*. Repr. in *I Can't Go On, I'll Go On*, ed. Richard Seaver, 589–604. New York: Grove Press.

Beckett, Samuel, and Georges Duthuit. 1965. "Three Dialogues." In *Samuel Beckett: A Collection of Critical Essays*, ed. Martin Esslin, 16–22. Englewood Cliffs, NJ: Prentice-Hall.

Begam, Richard. 1992. "Splitting the *Différance:* Beckett, Derrida and the Unnameable." *Modern Fiction Studies* 38 (Winter): 873–92.

Ben-Zvi, Linda. 1986. *Samuel Beckett*. Boston: Twayne Publishers.

Bishop, Tom. 1969. "Samuel Beckett." *Saturday Review* 52 (November): 26–27, 59.

Booth, Wayne. 1974. *A Rhetoric of Irony*. Chicago: University of Chicago Press.

———. 1983. "The Empire of Irony." *Georgia Review* 37 (Winter): 719–37.

Burke, Kenneth. 1969. *A Grammar of Motives*. Berkeley: University of California Press.

Connor, Steven. 1988. *Samuel Beckett: Repetition, Theory, and Text*. New York: Basil Blackwell.

Conquergood, Dwight. 1992. "Ethnography, Rhetoric, and Performance." *Quarterly Journal of Speech* 78:80–97.

Constantinidis, Stratos. 1993. *Theatre under Deconstruction? A Question of Approach.* New York: Garland Publishing.

Culler, Jonathan. 1982. *On Deconstruction: Theory and Criticism after Structuralism.* Ithaca, NY: Cornell University Press.

Dearlove, J. E. 1985. "Allusion to Archetype." *Journal of Beckett Studies* 10:121–33.

de Man, Paul. 1982. "The Resistance to Theory." *Yale French Studies* 63:3–20.

Derrida, Jacques. 1978. *Writing and Difference.* Chicago: University of Chicago Press.

———. 1982. *Dessemination.* Trans. Barbara Johnson. Chicago: University of Chicago Press.

Driver, Tom. 1961. "Beckett by the Madeline." *Columbia University Forum* 4 (Summer): 21–25.

Esslin, Martin. 1965. "Introduction." *Samuel Beckett: A Collection of Critical Essays,* ed. Martin Esslin, 1–15. Englewood Cliffs, NJ: Prentice-Hall.

Gontarski, S. E. 1983. "The Intent of Undoing in Samuel Beckett's Art." *Modern Fiction Studies* 29 (Spring): 5–23.

Hobson, Harold. 1956. "Samuel Beckett: Dramatist of the Year." *International Theatre Annual* 11:153–55.

Howard, Leigh Anne. 1995. "Boal and Theatre of the Oppressed: A Performance-Centered Inquiry of Eating and Body Image." Ph.D. diss., Louisiana State University.

Hutcheon, Linda. 1989. " 'Circling the Downspout of the Empire': Postcolonialism and Postmodernism." *Ariel* 20 (October): 149–79.

Juliet, Charles. 1989–90. "Meeting Samuel Beckett." Trans. and ed. Suzanne Chamier. *Tri-Quarterly* 11 (Winter): 9–30.

McCarthy, P. A. 1985. "Samuel Beckett: The Sense of Unending." *The Carrell* 23:1–24.

Osborn, Michael. 1976. "A Rhetorical Theory for Metaphor." Paper presented at the annual meeting of the Eastern Speech Association.

Pountney, Rosemary. 1988. *Theatre of Shadows: Samuel Beckett's Drama 1956–76.* Gerrards Cross, Buckinghamshire: Colin Smythe Ltd.

Rabinovitz, Rubin. 1992. *Innovation in Samuel Beckett's Fiction.* Urbana: University of Illinois Press.

Schneider, Alan. 1958. "Waiting for Beckett." *Chelsea Review* (Autumn): 3–20.

Scholes, Robert. 1988. "Deconstruction and Communication." *Critical Inquiry* 14:278–95.

Schusterman, Richard. 1988. "Croce on Interpretation: Deconstruction and Pragmatism." *New Literary Review* 20:199–216.

Webb, Eugene. 1982. *The Plays of Samuel Beckett.* Seattle: University of Washington.

Zurbrugg, Nicholas. 1990. "Seven Types of Postmodernism: Several Types of Samuel Beckett." In *The World of Samuel Beckett,* ed. Joseph H. Smith, 30–52. Baltimore: Johns Hopkins University Press.

Still Angry after All These Years:

Performing the Language of HIV

and the Marked Body in *The Normal*

Heart and *The Destiny of Me*

Peter Michael Pober

T IS 1 December 1995, World AIDS Day. Peter Jennings announces on the ABC News that AIDS is now the leading cause of death in Americans under the age of forty-five and that 70 percent of AIDS cases worldwide now occur in sub-Saharan Africa. This news does not change the perceptions, however. The audience is introduced to an American doctor from Lake Charles, Louisiana, who is living in South Africa, caring for HIV+ South Africans through the HOPE program. He explains that since the dissolution of the apartheid system, over 1.8 million South Africans have contracted HIV. Walking through the streets of Soweto Township, he speaks to many young black South Africans about HIV, about wearing a condom to protect themselves. In nearly every conversation, the young men respond, "Why, HIV is a white gay man's disease." It is 1995 and HIV is still perceived as a gay disease worldwide. But why?

In the United States, it would be easy to accuse the Centers for Disease Control and the media for constructing HIV as a gay disease. The CDC made the original link to "behaviors in homosexuals," announced the four primary risk groups (all marginalized to begin with), and refused to announce the "epidemic" until long after it had been confirmed. The argument would continue that the media wrote about "41 cases of rare cancer seen in homosexuals," shifted that to "gay cancer," from there joined forces with the CDC to speak about GRID (Gay Related Immune Deficiency) and created the homophobic panic that justified presumed deviance. By constructing binaries designed to exclude more at risk than are included, we have created a false sense of security; we have acquiesced to Michael Fumento's homophobic assumption that most Americans (read heterosexual) are not at risk for contracting HIV. Do not talk about it and it will not bother you. Do not address it and it will not appear. Indeed, the activists from ACT UP have been correct all along: Silence=Death. But unfortunately, death is allowable when those marginalized segments had been sick/diseased long before HIV and AIDS.

This essay will analyze (1) the use of the dichotomy between HIV+ and HIV–, (2) the concomitant development of a "Not Me" mentality regarding HIV, and (3) the changing identity of the HIV+ person during progressive stages of the virus. In each case I will then analyze the issue in terms of the autobiographical plays of Larry Kramer and others.

HIV+ Versus HIV–

Larry Kramer believes it, Robert Chesley believed it, Scott MacPherson spoke about it: HIV– individuals can never truly understand because they are not dying. The divisiveness of diagnosis is prevalent. Kramer sees "no way a healthy person can live with the feelings of those of us who are facing death, I'm sorry. And therein lies one of the major problems with all the AIDS organizations. They are run by do-gooders with all the time in the world to twiddle their thumbs while they spout pompous, pious odes to our illness" (quoted in Zonana 1992, 45). Lawrence Tate tells the story of one HIV+ friend who responds violently to an HIV– friend: "Oh shut up. Fuck you. You haven't got it. You don't know. You don't know shit" (1989, 63). David Black recounts similar reactions to his research from those in later stages of HIV: " 'You have no right,' he screamed, 'No right to do this story. . . .' 'Because I'm not gay?' I asked, ready to argue. But his answer was not what I'd expected. 'No,' he said, 'because you're not dying' " (1986, 31). But the argument is both isolationist and reductive. No, the respondent may not be dying of HIV, but to assume (1) that HIV– people cannot filter the suffering through other private experiences in their own lives, (2) that HIV– people cannot fight as successfully for the rights of people with AIDS, and (3) that HIV– people exhibit (at least partially) insincere empathy is to reduce the human capacity for both ethos and pathos immeasurably.

The reductive extension of this argument is that unless you specifically represent the biological and cultural categories presumed by the experience, you can never truly understand the experience. That is to say, if you are not a gay white Jewish male HIV+ New Yorker, you can never understand what Larry Kramer is going through. It is not only reductive to argue that; it is also isolationist. Especially is it so for Larry Kramer, who desires to be assimilated into heterosexualized performance of everyday life. His claiming that HIV– people cannot understand only serves to isolate him from the (presumed) healthy heterosexualized lifestyle that he so desires. Additionally, buttressing the HIV+ versus HIV– binary serves to isolate Kramer from the remainder of the gay population. Since he has always spoken of the need for unity within the "gay community," a unity which he believes will give "us" a voice in Washington, D.C., why then countermand that call to arms with an internally dichotomizing approach to HIV?

Kramer continues to contradict himself within his plays (given that his character Ned is the incarnate representation of Kramer). Prior to testing positive Ned reminds Felix that during the Nazi Holocaust American Jews did little to help Jews in Europe. He blames "Jewish organizations for constantly fighting among themselves" (1985, 50). Yet by constructing the HIV binary, he is doing the same thing. If Ned does not "want to be considered different" (57), why does he speak about being/feeling different? Is it not contradictory to accuse his brother Ben of "the single-minded determination of all you people to forever see us [homosexuals] as sick" (69) when he chooses to see himself as sick (and, as such, different)? And how can Ned justify his anger when Ben refuses to admit that heterosexuals and homosexuals are the same:

NED: I'm the same as you. Just say it. Say it!

BEN: No, you're not. I can't say it. (1.6.70)

If he concludes the scene with such vehemence that he "will not speak to you [Ben] until you accept me as your equal. Your healthy equal" (71), then how can he also see his HIV+ status as justification for not being the equal of an HIV– person? The experiences and perceptions of gays are culturally different from those of straights. Does it then follow that a gay person cannot understand how a straight person feels? In act two of *The Normal Heart* Ned angrily responds to the mayor's assistant, who finally meets with the GMHC representatives. Hiram, the mayor's spokesperson, notes "how impressed he [the mayor] is with your [homosexual] efforts to shoulder your own [homosexual] responsibility." Ned responds: "Our responsibility?" (86). If Ned is enraged because AIDS affects everybody, should he not also encourage those HIV– individuals to help if they desire to do so. Extending the linear

progression of this argument would mandate that since those HIV–
individuals could eventually test positive, just as other segments of the
population should take "responsibility," then they [the HIV–] should
be welcomed into the empathic communication model.

Examples in *The Destiny of Me* are also striking. In Ned's powerful
monologue early in act one, he asks, "What do you do when your own
people [gay men] won't unite and fight together to save their own
lives?" (Kramer 1993, 17). First, this question reconstructs HIV as a
gay disease. Second, Kramer is asking the entire "community" to unite
[HIV+ and HIV–], even though he sees the segmentation of understanding as irreconcilable and even though he only wants HIV– people
to help in a subjugated role. Toward the middle of act two Ned explains
to his younger self, Alexander, that in the coming out process, "You
want him [Ben] to understand. Oh, how you want him to understand!
He's not going to understand" (81). If Ben is not going to understand,
then how can Ned expect him to treat Ned as if they are "the same"?
At the end of act two Ned asks Ben, "Why was it so important to you
to make me the sick one?" (95). Is not Larry Kramer doing the exact
same thing with HIV?

This binary construction becomes equally unnerving in discussing
the performance of texts. If HIV– people can never truly understand
how the person with AIDS feels, would Larry Kramer insist that the
performer who portrays Ned in stage productions of these plays always
be HIV+ himself? Would not the argument that only the HIV+ truly
understand also apply to the ability of a performer to reconstruct the
biological and cultural categories inherent in the role? And since Larry
Kramer defines HIV as "our [the gay male population's] disease," surely
the performer should always be a gay man to truly understand the role.
All of this reductive and isolationist reasoning is contradictory to the
very foundation of performance, the attempt to raise consciousness of
an issue through the re-creation of perceived behaviors, language, and
paralinguistic cues that illuminate that issue. Indeed, only by inviting
the possibility of understanding can we hope to break down the binary
categories and allow for a broad range of experiences. This is precisely
what Victor Turner addresses: using performance in the process of social
healing. George Newtown explains: "In that process, marginal or liminal characters form a separate egalitarian and usually short-lived *communitas;* the secrets shared in the private enclave serve to heal the
greater society when the liminal figures are reintegrated into the social
structure" (1989, 220). Thus, it is because performance can bring to
light the thoughts and emotions, the suffering and fears, of the HIV+
that social awareness is possible. Witnessing the physical disintegration

and the emotional destruction caused by the virus, through the short-lived *communitas* constructed by the performance environment, then invites the possibility of understanding and social healing and encourages the reintegration of those with HIV into the social structure. This reintegration, then, to paraphrase Annette Martin, no longer allows anyone to leave free from understanding.

Not Me Mentality

Turn on the television. If we're shown a Gay Pride Parade, the camera zooms in on the transvestite, the leatherfolk, the drag queen. It is safe, sanitary for the heterosexual male who controls the gaze, because he knows that the marked image on the television could never be him: he could never be queer—he hates sequins. But in fact, beyond the binary that dichotomizes HIV+ from HIV– exists the underlying bifurcation of "us versus them" (read: straight versus gay). Filtered through images of fringe, multiple-marked elements of the "gay community," the heterosexist image-holder breathes a sigh of relief: "I can't get AIDS. That's not me."

The marked body becomes the conflated HIV+/gay body, a body feminized by the media and disempowered by its deviance from accepted heterosexual behaviors.[1] Hence comparative frameworks are created that define the intersignified HIV+/gay body only as it differs from the heterosexual body. Suzanne Pharr explains that gay men "are defined in relation to the norm and are found lacking. They are the Other. If they are not part of the norm, they are seen as abnormal, deviant, inferior, marginalized, not 'right' " (1988, 58). And this perception creates what David Black calls the "social immune system" (1986, 81), an us-versus-them construction that insures protection from HIV precisely because it insures protection from the breakdown of the heterosexual male body. That is to say, the heterosexual male becomes immune to HIV because his immune system is strong enough to prevent the preliminary breakdown which feminizes the body (because of homosexuality) in the first place. Critic Simon Watney explains that the "Spectacle

---

[1]Even in the case of the leatherfolk, the body is feminized because of the gay male's inability to actualize the behavior. That is to say, the macho performance fails to convince the heterosexist viewer of the heterosexualized behavior precisely because (1) the leatherfolk are shown in the context of the parade with other fringe elements, (2) the heterosexist viewer sees the macho behavior as mimicry, and as such, not completely credible, and/or (3) the leatherfolk behaviors appear exaggerated, hence unrealistic.

of AIDS," constructed by heterosexual/"Not Me" control of the gaze "ensure[s] that the subject of AIDS is 'correctly' identified and that any possibility of positive sympathetic identification with actual people with AIDS is entirely expunged from the field of vision. AIDS is thus embodied as an exemplary and admonitory drama" (1991, 78). Just like the "freak show" imagery presented by the media at a Gay Pride Parade, the heterosexist gaze confirms the abnormalities of the feminized gay or HIV+ body as similarly freakish. And Paula Treichler reminds us: "The text [of HIV] constructed around the gay male body . . . is driven in part by the need for constant flight from sites of potential identity and thus the successive construction of new oppositions that will barricade self from not-self" (1992, 65). In other words, the more heterosexist rhetoric and imagery can distance itself from potential conflation with the "sick" homosexual HIV+ body, the stronger the binary stands that constructs the "gay" disease. Each image that empowers the heterosexist gaze by adding to the list of unnatural behaviors associated with the marked body, disempowers and marginalizes the HIV+ ever more. Indeed, Treichler concludes, "Another appeal of thinking of AIDS as a 'gay disease' is that it protects not only the sexual practices of heterosexuality but also its ideological superiority" (49).

But the fault does not completely rest with the heterosexist rhetor and image-maker. Larry Kramer (and other gays, especially members of activist groups like ACT UP) have aided in the development of the us-versus-them binary. "Everyone in the government is the enemy and has been, at the city, state, and federal levels, across the board" (Pally 1990, 24). In like manner Larry Kramer declares, "Gay people have finally learned the terrible lesson that we are always going to have enemies no matter what" (quoted in Simpson, 7). And *New Republic* theatre critic Robert Brustein reminds us, "His [Kramer's] enemy is 'they'—the vast American majority that want to 'kill off all the faggots and niggers and spics' " (1992, 32). Brustein also insists, however, that Larry Kramer deliberately uses the performance of antagonism, constructing enemies through the development of binaries to "shame [his audience] into action" (32). Writing about the Broadway production of *The Destiny of Me,* Brustein claims that "Kramer's enemy is invariably the Other, and his constant purpose is to induce, excavate, and heighten the audience's sense of guilt" (32).

And Kramer does just that. Springboarding off his confrontational rhetoric that claims HIV– people can never truly understand the suffering of the HIV+, Larry Kramer makes the next inductive step in the argument. In a production titled *Indecent Materials,* staged in San Francisco in October 1992, the words of Larry Kramer are pitted against the words of North Carolina Senator Jesse Helms over the National Endowment for the Arts funding wars. Kramer's character retorts, "No heterosexual can understand what it's like to be a homosexual man today" (Winn 1992). And the stage is then set for both of Kramer's plays to present this binary.

Enter the Public Theatre in New York City for the 1985 production of *The Normal Heart* and one of the first things you see is the "number of cases [of AIDS] in gays [as distinct from] the number of cases in straights" on the theatre wall. The us-versus-them binary is established before the curtain even lifts. And but moments after it lifts, Dr. Brookner fears that nobody will do anything because "Who cares if a faggot dies?" (Kramer 1985, 34). Move to act one, scene six. Ben tells Ned, "It's your cause, not mine" (66). Kramer paints Ben as the heterosexual brother who buys into many of the media-constructed stereotypes of gay men. Failing to destigmatize the image-laden gay body, the body that was marked before AIDS, Ned tells Ben, "You know the media always dramatizes the most extreme. Do you think we all wear dresses . . . ?" (68). Ben responds, "Don't you?" (68). What Kramer does is reconfirm the traditional heterosexist projection of the gay body as already marked/feminized. Ned continues to bait Ben until Ben responds, "You make me sound like I'm the enemy" (71). Then Ned fires home: "I'm beginning to think that you and your straight world are our enemy" (71). The next tier of the binary is now established. Move to act one, scene eight. Dr. Brookner is yelling at Ned to get gay men to stop having sex. Ned asks, "How many of us [gay men] do you think already have the virus in our system?" (77). She responds, " . . . before a vaccine can be discovered almost every gay man will have been exposed" (77–78). Both maintain the safe zone for the heterosexual viewer, but Ned attacks: "What the fuck is your side doing? Where's the goddamned AMA in all of this? The government has not started one single test tube of research" (80). Larry Kramer may do little to deconstruct the HIV=gay relationship, but, as Robert Brustein noted, he does deliberately use his characters to induce guilt and shame. Moments later Ned tells Bruce, "They deny it's happening in straight people when it is" (82). But that is as far as he goes. And that may be the problem. Yes, the audience is shamed, but given the shoring up of the series of binaries now constructed—straight versus gay, us versus them, the straight medical establishment versus gay patients, the straight government versus the gay citizenry, and the HIV+/gay body versus the HIV−/straight body—one has to wonder if a little guilt and shame is enough. Ned concludes act two, scene ten, proclaiming, "We're being treated like shit. And we're allowing it. And until we force *them* to treat *us* [emphases mine] otherwise, we get exactly what we deserve" (91). This proclamation marks precisely the moment, for this writer, when Larry Kramer begins to turn the tables on the heterosexist stronghold because (1) he attempts to re-"masculinize" his rhetorical approach and (2) he is no longer willing to be the passive receiver. Near the conclusion of this monologue Ned bursts forth with one of Kramer's favorite retorts: "We're not yelling loud enough!" (91). And finally, Ned upsets the accepted role-projected behavior of a gay male by using heterosexist rhetoric to taunt Bruce, another gay man: "Bruce, for a Green Beret, you're an awful sissy!" (91). This is a bold rhetorical move for several reasons: (1) Ned is not joking; (2) he has taken an aggressive position, traditionally unacceptable but demystified in this context because it is toward another gay man; and (3) since Bruce exits the stage, leaving Ned alone (read temporarily victorious), he has established the "possibility" of heterosexualized behavior. The "possibility" exists, then, purely because Ned maintained his aggressive stance and survived, but the fact that it was the first step, and one addressed to another gay male, leaves us wondering if he will "survive and remain heterosexualized" when confronted by a "more worthy opponent."

The answer is no. Throughout the remainder of *The Normal Heart* Ned ostracizes himself for his inability to function within the group dynamic of the GMHC. He eventually leaves (primarily because his anger is no longer welcome) and becomes marked once again by the very behavior that has, since the Greeks, constructed effeminacy: "lack of control." Larry Kramer's deliberate reconstruction-in-performance of those binaries that he strives to eliminate in everyday interpersonal communication compromises the inclusivity of those bodies that could contract HIV. By striving for heterosexualized acceptance of homosexual relationships, while still politicizing the virus with gay rhetoric, Kramer reconfirms the heterosexist belief that (1) homosexuals are unsuccessful in their attempts to truly mimic "heterosexual" behaviors; (2) homosexual and heterosexual bodies are indeed different (the former marked, the latter unmarked); and (3) homosexuals, as already diseased (read compromised social immune systems), will continue to be the affected/infected group, maintaining a safe zone for the heterosexual body.

The television is turned off. The heterosexist gaze is protected. The binaries remain. That is Not Me. I would never behave like that.

Changing Identity for the HIV+

Michael Bronski paints an eerie end to the life of the marked body: "There are tubes and respirators, open sores and lesions, inflated and cooled mattresses to keep the fevers down to a manageable 103 degrees, balding due to chemotherapy, infections that coat the mouth and make it impossible to eat. Men who were once 200 pounds lie in bed reduced to 110-pound skeletons. Faces brimming with life and lust are reduced to courageous death masks animated only with the desire to live" (Bronski 1984, 141). These death masks mark the slipping away of lives begun with a series of masks (closeting both homosexuality and HIV), lives that used those masks to construct the erotic imagination and maintained them to act out its fantasies, lives destined to complete the masked/marked cycle in the same "deathbed" in which that cycle began.[2]

Diana Fuss believes that "sexual identity may be less a function of knowledge than performance, or, in Foucaultian terms, less a matter of final discovery than perpetual re-invention" (1991, 6–7). Given the continued conflation between sexuality and HIV, I see HIV identity in much the same way. Because the identity of the marked body becomes so determined by the progression of markings, the identity of the HIV+ individual is continuously in flux, perpetually reinventing itself. In essence, the question becomes, "How does 'I' (the body represented by the marked stages of HIV) perform 'I' (the identity of the individual)?" Or put more succinctly, what does it mean to perform HIV?

The changing identity of the HIV+ individual moves in stages: (1) fear of testing HIV+; (2) testing HIV+; (3) perceiving first externally visible physical signs; (4) inability to disguise physical markings any longer; (5) loss of physical recognition. Invoking the work of Jacques Lacan, one may say the mirror serves as the refractor of identity throughout the changing identity of the HIV+ person. Before the first physical markings of HIV appear, the diagnosed person searches for clues to changing identity: where will they appear, how quickly, and to what extent? Identity has already begun to shift because the HIV+ person no longer perceives him/herself in the same way. Andrew Holleran explains: "Your body—which you have tended, been proud of—is something you begin to view with suspicion, mistrust. . . . Your body could be harboring it, even as you go about your business. This keeps you on edge. You stop, for instance, looking in mirrors. Or at your body in the shower—because the skin, all of a sudden, seems as vast as Russia: a huge terrain, a monumental wall, on which tiny handwriting may sud-

---

[2]I use the term "deathbed" here to mean both the place of actual death and the place where the "death sentence" was exacted, the sexual bed in which the transmission of HIV occurred.

denly appear. The gums, the tongue, the face, the foot, the forearm, the leg . . . " (1989, 42–43).

The diagnosis begins to change the HIV+ person's identity, for one is no longer perceived as "healthy." Playwright Robert Chesley illuminates this attitudinal shift when he refers to his "Dog Plays," those plays written immediately after his diagnosis, as "my first AIDS plays" (1990, 122). Though he had written several AIDS texts prior to testing HIV+, Chesley, echoing the thoughts of Larry Kramer, appears to be saying that one can only truly understand HIV once one has been diagnosed: "Getting the diagnosis yourself thrusts you instantly out of the Golden Land of the (seemingly) Healthy, and into a different territory" (1990, 122). Larry Kramer concurs: "Suddenly knowing I'm HIV positive is very, very scary. It's made life exceedingly precious; it's made me work ten times harder on my work, my activism and writing. It's made me fight harder than ever in Washington. It's also made for bad dreams and horrors in the middle of the night" (quoted in Pally 1990, 86).

Finding that first visible lesion, catching a glimpse of lost weight, noticing white patches in the mouth, sweating at night, having a bit too much diarrhea—these are the signs of HIV, the signifying marked body no longer able to prevent the virus from showing itself. Notes one caller on an AIDS hotline, "It was, I thought, just a freckle on the inside of my arm. But it slowly got bigger, purplish" (Tate 1989, 57). And then he knew. Father Michael, the HIV+ priest in Victor Bumbalo's play *Show*, tells his orderly (the church has placed him in an institution because of his homosexuality and his HIV+ status), "I have a spot. A small purple spot. I'll show you. Here under my robes. With all its powerful meaning" (1992, 62–63). Indeed, Father Michael's identity is reconstituted by the appearance of the "small spot." Aware of what it entails, he hides the spot under his robes (in much the same way he hid his homosexuality) and will continue to do so until he no longer is able: "Before my spots double, triple. Before they devour me" (64).

Once the physical markings become overpowering, once the makeup will no longer cover the lesions, once the protein shakes will no longer bolster the weight, identity becomes reconstituted as "Not Me." The image which appears in the mirror is not clearly recognizable: the image, according to Robert Chesley, is that of an AIDS "ghost" or an AIDS "zombie." Buck, an HIV+ character in the later stages of AIDS in Chesley's play *(Wild) Person, Tense (dog)*, remarks " . . . I scarcely recognized *myself* when I looked into the mirror. Just couldn't believe it, you know?" (1990, 130). Indeed, the silence with which the Reagan and Koch administrations addressed the AIDS crisis in the first part of the plague could be said to have made the faces of the HIV+ unrecognizable to any of us. Individual identity is lost in the representation of HIV, replaced only by the lesion-covered face of the marked/gay/HIV+ body, a body represented, according to Richard Meyer, by the very "un-reality" (1991, 274) of being human. Frank Rich confirms this alienation when he speaks of Rock "the face of AIDS" Hudson's projected identity as a lie: "Everything that happened on screen was a lie, with the real content embedded in code" (1987, 100). By noting this, Rich has reconfirmed the formula of gay=sick, encouraged the belief that homosexuals are not to be trusted, and left his audience with the expectation that HIV will forge the true identity of the gay man, souring his looks and leaving him alienated and alien-like, as he deserves.

The final stage of the shifting identity of the HIV+ is literally the final stage of life. As with Holocaust victims, only some facial features remain distinguishable: "I dream of bodies stacked like those of the Holocaust and I recognize these faces," explains Marea Murray (1989, 170) as she walks through the AIDS ward of a hospital where she is visiting a friend. And the images identify the marked body as close to death: monitors, oxygen, intravenous tubes, until, to paraphrase playwright Robert Harling's character M'Lynn in *Steel Magnolias,* the breathing becomes slower and the beeps get farther apart; and then, no more (1988, 67).

In performances of both *The Normal Heart* and *The Destiny of Me,* Larry Kramer's characters portray the ever-changing identity of the HIV+ person. Critic Lianne Stevens of *The Los Angeles Times* noted in a review of the west coast production of *The Normal Heart:* "As Felix, McKenzie flirts, cajoles, charms and ultimately conveys the slow collapse of his body" (1986). And critic Hap Erstein wrote in his review for *The Washington Times* that Jonathan Hadary's performance of Ned Weeks in the Broadway production of *The Destiny of Me* made his body appear "close-cropped and frail-looking" (1992). But that may well be because Larry Kramer gave the performers a great deal to work with.

Throughout both plays Kramer gingerly supplies stage directions and dialogue that address the changing identities and performances of the marked body. The opening moment of *The Normal Heart* constructs the early fear and paranoia surrounding diagnosis and the first signs of HIV. Craig and Mickey sit in Dr. Brookner's waiting room:

CRAIG: Did you see that guy in there's spots?

MICKEY: You don't have those. Do you?

CRAIG: No.

MICKEY: Then you don't have anything to worry about.

CRAIG: She said they can be inside you, too. (1985, 31)

Here Larry Kramer clearly depicts the first move in the shifting identity of the HIV+ person: waiting for the first visible clue (often a KS lesion) and the fear and paranoia that accompany those reactions directly prior to diagnosis. Craig, however, already shows signs of HIV. He tells Mickey, "I'm tired all the time. I wake up in swimming pools of sweat. Last time she felt me and said I was swollen" (32). Craig is examined by Dr. Brookner, his fears are confirmed, and he exits her office radically altered: "I'm going to die. That's the bottom line of what she's telling me" (33). In act two, Felix is diagnosed with HIV. Upon hearing the confirmation from Dr. Brookner that he has caught it "early," Felix's identity, like Craig's before him, becomes enveloped in death: "It . . . takes longer until you die" (92). When the later stages of HIV occur, Bruce remembers that the person with AIDS is perceived as a "freak." As he tells the poignant story of trying to take his dying lover Albert back to Phoenix to be with his mother, Bruce remembers Albert becoming incontinent, "and all these people are staring at us and moving away in droves" (106), treating them like aliens. When they arrived in Phoenix, "the police are in complete protective rubber clothing, they looked like fucking astronauts" (106). Finally, after Albert dies, an orderly stuffs him in "a heavy-duty Glad Bag and . . . puts him out in the back alley with the garbage" (106). Alienation and worthlessness frame his story, reminiscent of the stacking of dead bodies in the Holocaust and the stigma associated with the "contagion" of both HIV and homosexuality. By scene fourteen of act two, Felix no longer recognizes himself in the mirror. He yells at Ned: "Don't touch me! I'm so ugly. I cannot stand it when you look at my body" (115). "Ned," Felix continues, "it's going to get messier any day now" (117). And confirming his presence in the later stages of HIV, he speaks of an acquaintance named David, who "finally died. He took forever. They say he looked like someone out of Auschwitz" (117). Felix, like so many in the concentration camps of World War II, doesn't want to fight anymore: "No!—I've had over forty treatments. No!—I've had three, no four different types of chemo. No!—I've had interferon, a coupla kinds. I've [even] had two different experimentals. I've had to go into the hospital four times—and please God don't make me go back into the hospital until I die. You cannot force the goddamn sun to come out" (117).

Felix has had enough: he has suffered nineteen months of tests and bloodletting, drugs and hospitals, nineteen months of watching the markings of his body "devour" his body; of reinventing his identity through each stage, from fear to anger, from hope to resignation. And now in the final hours of his life he has decided to take control one last time, to seize his identity back from the syndrome, to strip himself of the performance of HIV, even for just an instant. And to reinvent Felix Turner.

But as the stage directions indicate, only moments after Felix dies, "two orderlies enter and push the hospital bed . . . off stage" (122). For Ned Weeks, a Jewish man soon to uncover his own HIV+ status, the mirror becomes symbolic of identity even in death. According to Jewish tradition the mirrors are covered after a death to prevent the image of death from entering the home and being seen. The quick removal of Felix's body has denied Ned access to his own image of death, left him unable to reconcile the visibly altered and psychologically changed identity that the last stages of AIDS bring to bear. He is prevented, according to tradition, from looking into a mirror for the following week of mourning, beyond which he will symbolically (and, to some extent, physically) begin no longer to recognize himself.

Concluding Thoughts

The marked body is the disempowered body. Stripped of its capacity to appear normal, it is treated as elderly, near death, untouchable, diseased. The media's treatment of AIDS as a "gay cancer" and the government's avoidance of the crisis struck panic in the public, encouraging the further marginalizing of the already marginalized. AIDS became a lesson to be taught, helping to prevent the "choice" of homosexuality, to choose health instead. And through each stage of misinformation and discrimination, the HIV+ body became more and more conflated with the gay body, with the marginalized body, with the disempowered body, until the binaries solidified and the "epidemic of signification" bifurcated the nation. Even in the cases of heterosexual transmission (e.g., Magic Johnson), the media continued to plant questions of a homosexual "cause."

The marked body becomes both an indicator of contagion (physical and psychological) and a justification for homophobia. Through performative images, the concept of contagion (as it relates to HIV and homosexuality) broadens to address the contagion of ideas, the belief that the mind is presumed ill and could infect others. Many people (both homosexual and heterosexual) saw the virus as reason to marginalize the gay population once again. This writer believes that the "infection" of ideas encouraged through the plays of Larry Kramer has in many ways been beneficial, for to infect someone with knowledge designed to clarify issues of disempowerment is to encourage everyone to address the plague appropriately. Larry Kramer, then, as the most performed playwright writing about HIV, has greatly "infected" those audience members who have witnessed one of the over six hundred productions of *The Normal Heart* and any of the more than one hundred productions of *The Destiny of Me*. Through performance of suffering and attempts to dissuade the fear of contagion, Kramer has prevented any of his audience members from leaving the theatre "free."

De-masculinizing rhetoric has "woman-ized" the marked body in an effort to show that the HIV+ person allowed or even encouraged the virus's transmission. Painting the HIV+ marked body as passive receiver of the virus confirms the notion that effeminacy means simply "lack of control." Larry Kramer refuses to accept that. In fact, Kramer deconstructs the sissification of the gay/HIV+ marked body through his angry rhetoric and scathing performance indictments. He speaks of the "need to yell louder," striving to "re-masculinize" the disempowered body. Although Kramer's screaming has drawn attention to the AIDS crisis, however, his behavior is still seen at times as trying to heterosexualize the "gay community," and unable to completely "pass" for the unmarked empowered body, he is left still arguing as a gay/HIV+ marked body.

Larry Kramer's work speaks powerfully about the tragedy of HIV and the suffering of those who are HIV+. But his insistence on an us-versus-them mentality has done nothing to pull apart the binaries being constructed. In fact, he has strengthened them by focusing on what "they" did to "us." Larry Kramer is guilty of buttressing the HIV+ versus HIV− binary through his assessment that an HIV− person can never truly understand what he and other HIV+ persons are going through.

Larry Kramer's treatment of HIV in his autobiographical plays performs volumes, reminding all of us of the "power of theatrical performance to intervene effectively in social issues" (Strine, 393–94). He blasted the media for its misinformation, heckled the government for its silence, and pricked the medical community for its inaction. And he did this through performance, the performance of activism (ACT UP), the performance of propaganda (his editorials everywhere), and the performance of his plays. Although Larry Kramer did little (if anything) to countermand the comparative binaries established through this "plague of representations," his plays and activism present the image of the marked body placed in the context of life experience: "*The Normal Heart* did mark a sociopolitical if not a creative breakthrough, and there is no question that it helped propel discussion of the disease into public discourse" (Caldwell 1990, 344).

It is Larry Kramer's hope that "the writing on the theater's [and extradiegetic] walls alone could drive anyone with a normal heart to abandon the million excuses for not getting involved" (Rich, 1985, C17).

Works Cited

Black, David. 1986. *The Plague Years: A Chronicle of AIDS, the Epidemic of Our Times.* New York: Simon and Schuster.

Bronski, Michael. 1984. *Culture Clash: The Making of Gay Sensibility.* Boston: South End Press.

———. 1989. "Death and the Erotic Imagination." In *Personal Dispatches: Writers Confront AIDS,* ed. John Preston, 133–44. New York: St. Martin's Press.

———. 1989. "AIDS, Art and Obits." In *Personal Dispatches: Writers Confront AIDS,* ed. John Preston, 161–66. New York: St. Martin's Press.

Brustein, Robert. 1992. "The Editorial Play." *New Republic,* 7 Dec., 32–34.

Bumbalo, Victor. 1992. "Show." *Tough Acts to Follow,* ed. Noreen C. Barnes and Nicholas Deutsch. San Francisco: Alamo Square Press. 59–68.

Caldwell, Mark. 1990. "The Literature of AIDS: Sensationalism, Hysteria, and Good Sense. *Dissent* 37 (Summer): 342–47.

Chesley, Robert. 1990. *Hard Plays/Stiff Parts.* San Francisco: Alamo Square Press.

Erstein, Hap. 1992. " 'Destiny': Rage Tempered by Hope." *Washington Times,* 28 Oct., sec. B, p. 9.

Fuss, Diana, ed. 1991. *inside/out.* New York: Routledge.

Harling, Robert. 1988. *Steel Magnolias.* New York: Dramatists Play Service.

Holleran, Andrew. 1989. "The Fear." In *Personal Dispatches: Writers Confront AIDS,* ed. John Preston, 38–46. New York: St. Martin's Press.

Kramer, Larry. 1985. *The Normal Heart.* New York: New American Library.

———. 1993. *The Destiny of Me.* New York: Penguin Books.

Meyer, Richard. 1991. "Rock Hudson's Body." *inside/out,* ed. Diana Fuss, 259–88. New York: Routledge.

Murray, Marea. 1989. "All Too Familiar." In *Personal Dispatches: Writers Confront AIDS,* ed. John Preston, 167–71. New York: St. Martin's Press.

Newtown, George. 1989. "Sex, Death, and the Drama of AIDS." *Antioch Review* 47 (Spring): 209–22.

Pally, Marsha. 1990. "AIDS Activism: A Conversation with Larry Kramer." *Tikkun* 5 (July–August): 22–24, 84–87.

Pharr, Suzanne. 1988. *Homophobia: A Weapon of Sexism.* Inverness, CA: Chardon Press.

Rich, Frank. 1985. "Theater: *The Normal Heart,* by Larry Kramer." *New York Times,* 22 April, sec. C, p. 17.

———. 1987. "The Gay Decades." *Esquire,* November, 99.

Simpson, Janice C. 1990. "Using Rage to Fight the Plague." *Time,* 5 Feb, 7–8.

Stevens, Lianne. 1986. "Powerful Story Beats in *The Normal Heart.*" *Los Angeles Times* 14 Oct., sec. 6, p. 1.

Strine, Mary S. 1992. "Art, Activism, and the Performance (Con)Text: A Response." *Text and Performance Quarterly* 12:391–94.

Tate, Lawrence. 1989. "The Epidemic: A San Francisco Diary." In *Personal Dispatches: Writers Confront AIDS,* ed. John Preston, 53–71. New York: St. Martin's Press.

Treichler, Paula A. 1992. "AIDS, HIV, and the Cultural Construction of Reality." In *Time of AIDS: Social Analysis, Theory, and Method,* ed. Gilbert Herdt and Shirley Lindenbaum, 65–98. Newbury Park: Sage.

Watney, Simon. 1991. "The Spectacle of AIDS." In *AIDS: Cultural Analysis: Cultural Activism,* ed. Douglas Crimp, 71–86. Cambridge, MA: MIT Press.

White, Edmund. 1989. "Esthetics and Loss." In *Personal Dispatches: Writers Confront AIDS,* ed. John Preston, 145–52. New York: St. Martin's Press.

———. 1991. "Out of the Closet, onto the Bookshelf." *New York Times,* 10 June, 22, 24, 35.

Winn, Steven. 1992. " 'Indecent Materials' Pits Kramer Against Helms." *San Francisco Chronicle,* 21 Oct., Daily Datebook, sec. E, p. 1.

Zonana, Victor. 1992. "Kramer vs. the World." *Advocate,* 1 Dec., 40–48.

Contributors

John Arthos is Assistant Professor of Communications at SUNY Fredonia. His research on narrative art has appeared in *The Journal of Narrative Technique, Film and Philosophy,* and *Classical Heritage.* His documentary films on culture and education are distributed by Cinema Guild, Filmmakers Library, and Meridien Entertainment.

George L. Geckle is Professor of English at the University of South Carolina, Columbia, South Carolina. He is editor of *Twentieth Century Interpretations of "Measure for Measure"* and the author of *John Marston's Drama: Themes, Images, Sources* and *"Tamburlaine" and "Edward II": Text and Performance.* He has also published many articles on Shakespeare and other Elizabethan and Jacobean dramatists.

Tom Heeney is Assistant Professor of Communication at the College of Charleston, South Carolina. His research interests include rhetorical theory, philosophy, aesthetics, and literature. He has published articles or book reviews in *Philosophy and Rhetoric, The Quarterly Journal of Speech,* and *The Personalist Forum.*

Leigh Anne Howard is Codirector and Assistant Professor of Communication at Spalding University in Louisville, Kentucky. Several of her articles have received awards at the Southern States Communication convention and have been published in *Theatre Insight, Behavioral Scientist,* and *Organizational Advocacy: Rhetoric in the Information Age.*

She is also former editor of *The Center,* a performing arts magazine in Louisville.

Odai Johnson teaches at Southwestern Missouri State University. His articles on Restoration theatre have appeared in *Theatre Journal* and *Theatre Survey.*

Stanley Vincent Longman is Professor of Drama at the University of Georgia. He has published a book on dramatic writing titled *Composing Drama for Stage and Screen.* He has also published articles on the Italian theatre of the modern times and of the Renaissance. He has translated several plays by such playwrights as Carlo Goldoni, Luigi Pirandello, Pier Maria Rosso di San Secondo, Luigi Antonelli, and Dino Buzzati.

Peter Michael Pober is a faculty member in the Department of Speech Communication at the University of Texas at Austin. He directs the university's nationally ranked Individual Events Program and its National Institute in Forensics. Students in the University of Texas Forensics Union, which he codirects, have been awarded the American Forensic Association's Overall National Championship in Speech and Debate for the last four consecutive years.

Maria Galli Stampino received her Ph.D. in Italian and Comparative Literature from Stanford University in 1996. She is currently Assistant Professor of Italian and French at the University of Miami. She is at work on a book on Torquato Tasso's pastoral *Aminta;* she has published on theatre and issues of representation in *Quaderni d'italianistica* and *Romance Review.*

August W. Staub is Professor Emeritus of Drama at the University of Georgia, where he chaired the Department of Drama for nineteen years. His books include *Creating Theatre* and *Varieties of Theatrical Art.* He has published over fifty articles in scholarly journals.

Charles Wilbanks teaches speech at the University of South Carolina in the Department of Theatre, Speech and Dance. He is the author of *The Dynamics of Public Speaking* and *Speaking Out!: Rights, Responsibilities and Process of Public Speech.* He is coauthor of *Values and Policies in Controversy.*

Steve Wilmer teaches at Trinity College Dublin, where he has been Director of the Samuel Beckett Centre for Drama and Theatre Studies. He was recently a Visiting Professor in the Department of Drama at Stanford University. He has written on Irish and American Drama and is also a playwright. His play *Scenes from Soweto* was published in *Best Short Plays of 1979*.